Heart of Darkness

JOSEPH CONRAD

Level 5

Retold by Nancy Taylor
Series Editors: Andy Hopkins and Jocelyn Potter

Pearson Education Limited
Edinburgh Gate, Harlow,
Essex CM20 2JE, England
and Associated Companies throughout the world.

ISBN: 978-1-4058-8245-3

First published 2007
This edition published 2008

3 5 7 9 10 8 6 4

Set in 11/14 Bembo
Printed in China
SWTC/03

Published by Pearson Education Limited in association with
Penguin Books Ltd, both companies being subsidiaries of Pearson PLC

Acknowledgements
Every effort has been made to trace the copyright holders and we apologise in advance
for any unintentional omissions. We would be pleased to insert the appropriate
acknowledgement in any subsequent edition of this publication.

We are grateful to the following for permission to reproduce this photograph:
Natural Science Photos: pgx (©Clive Jones)
Picture research by Lisa Wren/Sandra Hilsdon

For a complete list of the titles available in the Penguin Readers series please write to your local
Pearson Longman office or to: Penguin Readers Marketing Department, Pearson Education,
Edinburgh Gate, Harlow, Essex CM20 2JE

Contents

Introduction

'Kurtz lay on his bed staring but not seeing. He could not see me or the wall or the curtain, but he could see the whole universe; he could see clearly into every heart that beat in the darkness. He made his judgement on the world: "The horror!"'

Heart of Darkness is the story Charlie Marlow tells his four friends, who have all worked at sea, about his job several years earlier as a steamboat captain on the River Congo. But as the friends listen, they – and we – realise that this is not an ordinary story about working on an unfamiliar river. Instead, it is a story of the battle in each man's soul when he looks at the unfamiliar dark centre of his heart and discovers his own truth.

The background to the story was popular news towards the end of the nineteenth century, when most of Africa was divided into colonies owned by European countries. The very large area known as the Congo Free State became a Belgian colony in 1885 after King Leopold II learned about the unbelievable riches, especially ivory and rubber, that European powers could take advantage of. A colony for Leopold meant a place where he could easily change the natural products into wealth by using black slave workers under the direction of a few white managers and agents. At home in Europe the King, who never visited Africa, advertised his country's work in the Congo as scientific, kind and Christian. In reality he destroyed the society that existed there, and killed thousands, perhaps millions, of native Africans during Belgium's rule.

When Conrad was a boy in the 1860s and 1870s, much of Africa remained unexplored, but when he went there as a man in 1890 he saw that this enormous 'space' had been turned into a place of darkness by the European colonists. In the novel, Conrad clearly attacks nineteenth-century colonial attitudes and practices; Marlow's thoughts show the reader who Conrad judges to be guilty of misusing their power. But the story also goes beyond a historical picture of the situation and becomes a psychological exploration of the human heart.

At the centre of Marlow's story is the mysterious, extraordinary Mr Kurtz. We learn about his journey to the heart of darkness by hearing what other people tell Marlow about him, and finally by witnessing the meeting between the two men and hearing Kurtz's final judgement: 'The horror!' Conrad does not allow his readers to be certain of what Kurtz's final words mean to Marlow, or even to Kurtz himself, but he allows us, with Marlow, to struggle in trying to understand the difficult and complicated workings of the human mind.

Józef Teodor Konrad Korzeniowski was born in Berdyczów, Poland on 8 December 1857 into a well-educated upper-class family. It was important to Józef's future career, and to his future health, that his father and mother, as well as his uncles, aunts and cousins, were politically very active. At the time of Józef's birth, that part of Poland was controlled by Russia, and the adult members of the boy's family not only opposed this rule, but also actively fought against it; they wanted Poland to be independent of foreign control.

In 1861, Józef's father, a writer and translator, was put in prison and his land was taken from him as punishment for his part in a rebellion against Russian rule. Apollo Korzeniowski, his wife and their young son were sent to a distant Russian area where they suffered from poor health and difficult working conditions. Eva, Józef's mother, died there in 1865, and his father died soon after returning to Poland in 1869. Poland eventually became independent in 1919 as a result of the long fight carried out by people like Józef's family, but the young boy, like many other children, was now an orphan in poor health, which he suffered from during his whole life. This background prepared Józef to be sympathetic to weak people who suffered under the unfair control of powerful rulers.

The twelve-year-old orphan was brought up by his mother's brother, Thaddeus Bobrowski, a kind, practical man. He put Józef into good schools and provided him with private teachers, but the boy was a poor student and never completed his formal course of studies in Greek, Latin, mathematics and geography. But this lack of interest in school did not stop Józef from learning about the world. He read translations of Charles Dickens and other English novels, especially books by Captain Frederick Marryat about life at sea, and he read widely in French, including such books as Victor Hugo's *Workers of the Sea*, which Conrad described as 'my first introduction to the sea in literature'. These books, as well as maps of unexplored places, excited him about the idea of travel and especially about sea voyages, and at sixteen he decided that he wanted to find work on a ship and see the world.

In 1874, Józef went to Marseille and joined the French commercial navy, working for them on ships until 1878 and enjoying the seafront life around the port. But in that year he tried to kill himself, possibly because he was depressed about his heavy debts, or because he did not want to return to Poland and join the army there. But he lived and, with the help of his uncle, he moved on to England and joined the crew of the *Mavis*, a ship in the British commercial navy, which he stayed with for less than a year. After he left, he enjoyed a rather wild life in London until his uncle persuaded him to return to the ships and become serious about his career. It is worth noting that at this point in his life, at the age of twenty, Józef said of himself that he knew only six words of English.

In sixteen years as a seaman on British ships, Józef travelled to places as far away as Bangkok, Singapore and Australia, although later he wrote that he hated the day-to-day life of a sailor. However, he obtained his master's certificate (which meant he could be a ship's captain) in the commercial navy and also became a British citizen in 1886.

One of his last journeys, especially important to his future career as a writer, was on a steamboat up the River Congo in 1890. He had read the reports of European trading activities in that region and looked for a job there for adventure and to make money. He witnessed extraordinary cruelty towards the native Africans and was discouraged by the Europeans' reasons for being there. *Heart of Darkness* first appeared in 1902, and in an introduction to it, written in 1917, Conrad wrote that the book '... is experience pushed a little (and only very little) beyond the actual facts of the case.' As you read the novel, it is important to remember that the main character witnesses the kind of activities and meets the kind of people that Conrad saw in 1890.

By the time *Heart of Darkness* was written, Józef Teodor Konrad Korzeniowski was Joseph Conrad, the writer. He chose to use this name when he produced his first novel, *Almayer's Folly*, in 1895. In the year after that he married Jessie George and wrote his second novel, followed quickly by several more books. However, he was not successful as a popular novelist until 1913 when he wrote *Chance,* one of many novels with the sea as background. This book finally brought him financial success as well as the respect he had already earned for the quality of his writing.

Conrad took ideas for many of his novels from his experience at sea as well as from the political ideas that he learned from his family. But most importantly, he often examines in his books the lives of characters who live in a difficult, unsympathetic world in which their morals and beliefs are tested. In *Lord Jim* (1900), for example, Conrad writes about a cowardly act and how it affects the main character for the rest of his life; this story is told by Charlie Marlow, the character who returns as the storyteller in

Heart of Darkness. In *Chance* Conrad looks at the ways an innocent person is changed by the horrific world she lives in; *Nostromo* (1904) examines an individual's social and political life in a South American country; *The Secret Agent* (1907) centres around a plot to bomb London and destroy the government. His later works continue to examine the changing nature of truth and of the modern human character, and consider the frightening idea that all human beings are separate and alone.

For the last ten years of his life Joseph Conrad continued to write and enjoy financial success. He died of heart failure on 3 August 1924 in England, and was buried in Canterbury Cathedral.

Conrad is still considered to be one of the greatest modern writers because his work makes readers question their own beliefs, as well as the beliefs and practices of their country and of the outside world. As a writer, he has been described as an Impressionist because he brings to light the dreams and emotions in each of his character's private view of reality. This is especially true of *Heart of Darkness*, which holds a mirror up to the weaknesses in every human soul.

Readers of *Heart of Darkness* may also be interested in the most famous film based on the novel: *Apocalypse Now* (1979). The director, Francis Ford Coppola, uses the idea of a journey up river during the war in Vietnam to find an army officer named Kurtz. Like Conrad's Kurtz, this man has broken away from the rules he has agreed to follow and has become a god to the natives around him. The film does not follow the novel in every detail, but it creates a similar mysterious, horrifying atmosphere and, like the novel, it leaves the viewer with unanswered questions about every individual's role in life.

'Would this land and this river control us or would we control them?'

Chapter 1 Travelling to the Heart of Darkness

The *Nellie*, a small sailing ship, dropped her anchor and rested quietly on the calm waters of the River Thames. There was almost no wind, and since we were travelling down the river, we could only wait for the tide to turn and carry us towards the sea.

We could see the mouth of the Thames stretching in front of us like the beginning of an endless waterway. In the distance the sky ran into the sea, and in the brilliant light we could see other boats floating up towards us with the tide, their sails looking sharp and shiny red in the afternoon sun. Behind us the air was dark above Gravesend, more than forty kilometres to the west, and further away there seemed to be a sad, grey cloud hanging unmoving over the biggest, and the greatest, town on earth: London.

The Director of Companies was our captain and our host. The other four of us on board watched him affectionately as he stood at the front of the boat looking out to sea. On the whole river there was nobody who looked so completely like a sailor. It was difficult to understand, even knowing our situation, why his work was not out there on the bright sea instead of behind us on the darkness of the Thames.

The sea was the chain that held the five of us together, even through long periods of separation, making us accept each other's stories, feelings and beliefs. The Lawyer, the oldest of us, had the only cushion and was lying comfortably on the only piece of carpet. The Accountant was checking the pieces of a game he had brought along to make the time pass more quickly, and Marlow sat at the back on the hard floor, leaning against a pole. He had a thin face, yellow skin, a straight back, and the look of a poet or philosopher.

1

The Director, having checked that the boat would not move, finally came and sat down, and all five of us fell into a comfortable silence, each of us staring calmly at the peaceful water and the gentle sky, full of clear light. Even the misty air on the riverbanks gave the impression of a thin, shiny material hanging beautifully at the water's edge. Only the darkness in the west was becoming more threatening, giving the impression that it was angered by the approach of the setting sun.

At last the sun sank low, and its colour changed from brilliant white to a dull red with neither brightness nor heat. Immediately, a change came over the water around us, and the peace and quiet became less brilliant but deeper. The old river rested untroubled at the end of the day, after centuries of good service to the people who used it.

The Thames was confident in its power; it was a river which led to every corner of the earth. We looked at this great waterway through the light of its history, and for men who have 'followed the sea' with love and respect, nothing can bring the spirit of the past to mind as easily as the Thames. This great river was crowded with the memories of men going to battle, hoping to discover new lands, planning to make their fortunes, and returning home rich, victorious, and with knowledge of a new world. The Thames had known the ships and the men. Hunters for gold or chasers after fame, they had all gone out on that river, carrying the dreams of men and beliefs and ideas from their homeland to faraway countries.

The sun set and lights began to appear along the shore as the lamps of ships moved up and down the river under the stars.

'And this,' said Marlow suddenly, 'has also been one of the dark places on the earth.'

Charles Marlow was the only man of us who still 'followed the sea', but he was different from other sailors. Most seamen want a quiet life; their home – the ship – is always with them, and so is their country – the sea. One ship is very similar to any other, and the sea is always the same. Sailors are not very interested in foreign lands or foreign faces, which cannot compare to the wonderful mysteries of the sea. But Marlow was not typical: his interests went beyond the sea; he was curious about the world, and especially about people.

His remark did not surprise us. It was typical of Marlow, and we accepted it in silence. He continued slowly, 'I was thinking of very old times, when the Romans first came here, nineteen hundred years ago, but it seems like yesterday. Darkness was here then. Imagine a Roman commander on his ship in the Mediterranean Sea. He receives orders to go north, across land and sea, here, to the end of the world. He finds a grey sea, a sky the colour of smoke, and this river. He sees wild men and finds nothing for a man of culture to eat or drink. Cold, fog, storms, disease and death hang in the air, waiting in the water and in the forests. His men die like flies here, but they are brave enough to face the darkness. And maybe the commander is ambitious and, if he does not die here, hopes he will be sent to a nice sunny place near Rome, with good food and drink, and be surrounded by pleasant, educated people.

'Or imagine a fine young Roman coming here to make his fortune as a trader or a tax-collector, perhaps to pay his debts. The cruelty and wildness around him swallows him up. The mysterious life that exists in the forest, in the hearts of wild men, destroys him. There is no way to be prepared for such a situation. You have to live in the middle of it, and although it is ugly and beyond your experience or imagination, it also attracts you, pulls you in. Imagine the regrets, the desire to escape, the powerless disgust, the surrender, the hate.'

He paused.

'Of course,' he began again, 'none of us would feel exactly like this. We are saved by our commitment to efficiency. But the

Romans were not interested in running a country; they wanted wealth, profit. They seized what they could get by using force; it was murder and robbery with violence, which is the way for people who have to fight a darkness. Conquest of the earth, which mostly means taking it away from people with a different coloured skin or flatter noses, is not admirable when you think about it carefully. It is rescued by an idea. An unselfish belief in an idea – something you can believe in, and offer a sacrifice to …'

He stopped speaking. The traffic of the great city continued on the sleepless river as the night grew darker. We watched, waiting patiently – there was nothing else to do until the tide changed. After a long silence, Marlow said, uncertainly, 'I once spent some time away from the sea. I was a riverboat captain, as I'm sure you remember.' We knew then that before we continued our journey on the *Nellie,* we were going to hear about one of Marlow's strange adventures.

◆

'I do not want to bore you with what happened to me personally,' Marlow began, seeming to forget that personal experiences interest audiences the most. 'But to understand the effect on me of my riverboat days, you ought to know some details of how I got there, what I saw, and where I first met Kurtz, the poor man at the centre of my story. That meeting seemed somehow to throw a kind of light on everything around me, and into my thoughts. It was a sad meeting, too, not extraordinary in any way, and not very clear either. No, not clear, but it seemed to throw a kind of light.

'As you remember, I returned to London after six years or more on the Indian Ocean, the Pacific, the China Seas, and I was lazy for some time, staying at your houses, preventing you working, trying to educate you about the East. Of course, eventually I got tired of resting and began the difficult job of finding a ship, but no one wanted me.

'When I was a young boy, maps excited me. I looked for hours at South America, or Australia, or the North Pole, and lost myself in the excitement of exploration. I particularly loved the big, empty spaces where no European had discovered a river or named a mountain. I often placed my finger on one of these unexplored areas and said, "When I grow up, I will go there." And there was one place – the biggest and the emptiest – which attracted me more than all the others: Africa.

'I found myself on a street in London looking at a map of Africa in a shop window. It is true that in the years since my childhood, the continent had filled up with the names of rivers, lakes and mountains. It was not a mysterious, empty white space for me to dream about. It had become a place of darkness. But there was still something that captured my imagination. I stared at a big, powerful river that, like an enormous snake, stretched its head out into the sea as its body curved great distances across the land to its tail. Suddenly, I remembered an important company that traded on that river. "Stop and think!" I said to myself. "They can't have a trading company without using some kind of riverboat – steamboats, of course!" The snake had charmed me, and I hurried off to find a job on the River Congo.

'I was not successful until I wrote to a dear old aunt who had contacts in Belgium. She answered my letter saying, "I would be delighted to do anything I can for you – anything! I will speak to a few important friends who I am sure will help."

'With my aunt's recommendation I got my appointment very quickly. In fact, the Company had received news that one of their captains, a Dane named Freslaven, had recently been killed in a quarrel with the natives.

'Months later, when I tried to find Freslaven's body, I heard more of the details of the argument, which began as a misunderstanding about chickens. It appeared that Freslaven believed he had been cheated and without warning started to beat the chief of the village with a stick. A crowd gathered to watch Freslaven – who was described as quiet and gentle, but perhaps dissatisfied with the lack of respect shown to him – as he beat the old man quite cruelly. Finally, the chief's son tried to stop Freslaven by gently pushing the Dane in the back with his spear. Sadly the weapon slipped in between the bones of his shoulders and killed the man. The whole population of the village disappeared immediately into the forest and Freslaven's steamboat left just as quickly with the frightened engineer at the wheel. Later, when I had the opportunity, I found the empty village – no people or chickens had returned – and Freslaven's body with tall grass growing between his bones.

'Because of the Freslaven affair, I was needed immediately. I made my preparations quickly, and in less than forty-eight hours I was crossing the English Channel to meet my employers and to sign my contract in Brussels. The Company was easy to find since it was the most important in town and everybody was talking about it. The Company's goal was to run a great trading business abroad and make an enormous pile of money.

'I passed through large double doors and up a staircase, and opened the first door I came to. Two women, one fat and the other thin, both dressed in very plain clothes, sat on simple, low chairs, knitting black wool. The thin one stood up and walked straight towards me, keeping her eyes on her knitting. She only looked up and stopped at the last moment before crashing into me. She turned round without a word and led me into a waiting room, with a big shiny map of Africa on one wall. There was a large amount of red on the map marking Great Britain's possessions, plus a lot of blue for France, a little green for Italy, some orange for Portugal, and a small spot of purple for Germany. However, I was not going to any of these places. I was going into the yellow area right in the centre, owned by Belgium. And the river was there – amazing – deadly – like a snake! I was shown into a grand office and forty-five seconds later, after meeting the great man himself and signing my contract, I was in the waiting room again.

'I had had an uncomfortable feeling while I was in the office that something was not quite right. I did not know what it was, but the atmosphere was secretive, and I was glad to get back into the outer room where the two women continued to knit. The thin, younger one led more people into the waiting room, while the older one sat in her chair with a cat resting in the folds of her dress. Her look seemed to say that she knew everything about me and about everyone else who passed through these offices. There was something mysterious and powerful about her, and she frightened me. Often, when I was far away from Brussels, I thought of these two, guarding the door of Darkness, knitting black wool, one introducing men to an unknown world, the other examining each new face with her wise, old eyes. Not many of the men she looked at ever saw her again.

'I left the Company's offices with one final piece of business to complete: a visit to the doctor who would decide if I was fit for the job. The doctor listened to my heart while obviously thinking about something else. "Good, good for out there," he said without much interest, and then in a much more enthusiastic voice, asked me if he could measure my head. Rather surprised, I agreed, and he took out his instruments and began measuring my head from every direction, taking careful notes as he did it. He was a harmless old fool, untidy in a thin, cheap coat, and I'm sure he had not shaved or bathed in days.

"I always ask permission to measure the heads of the men who are going out there," he said.

"And when they come back too?" I asked.

"Oh, I never see them," he remarked; "and, anyway, the changes take place inside their heads, you know." He smiled at a private joke. "Has there ever been any madness, any mental illness in your family?" he asked in a friendly way.

'I felt very annoyed. "Is that question in the interests of science too?"

"Well, I have a theory which I think you gentlemen who go out there could help me prove. Others can have the riches that my country will get from our foreign possessions, but I want scientific facts. And you are of special interest because you are the first Englishman who has been sent to me."

"I don't think I'm a typical example."

'He laughed and said, "That sounds wise, but is probably wrong. Anyway, my advice to you is to avoid mental upset even more than strong sunlight. In tropical climates you must, more than everything else, keep calm. Remember that. Goodbye."

'Back in England, one more thing remained for me to do: to say goodbye to my excellent aunt. We celebrated her success at finding me a job with a cup of tea, my last good cup of tea for many days, and we had a long chat beside the fire in her beautiful sitting room. As we talked, it became clear to me that she had painted a rather attractive picture of me to various important people. I was a talented, intelligent gentleman with many fine gifts, a person the Company would be very fortunate to have, the kind of man you do not find every day. But I was only going to be the captain of a small, shaky, old river-steamboat, with a cheap whistle to announce its arrival.

'According to my aunt's exaggerated description, I was an honourable man, someone who would help to change the world and spread not only the English way of life, but also the word of God. The newspapers had recently been full of this sort of idea, and my aunt found it attractive, and so talked about saving the uneducated natives from their savage ways. I began to feel quite uncomfortable and tried to remind her that the goal of the Company was to make a profit. But, like most women, she had little knowledge of the realities of business.

'I do not know why, but as soon as I was in the street I had the feeling that my plans, my ideas, everything about me was false. In the past I had always been able to prepare for a trip to anywhere in the world in twenty-four hours and without a second thought. But now, at least for a moment, I felt that, instead of going to the centre of a continent to begin a normal job, I was beginning a journey to the centre of the earth where something unusual waited for me.

◆

'I left in a French steamboat which stopped in every little port along the west coast of Africa for the purpose of leaving soldiers and customs officers there. I watched the coast, which is always like trying to solve a puzzle. There it is in front of you, giving you opposite signals: smiling, unfriendly, inviting, mean, grand, weak, strong, wild, and always whispering, "Come and find out."

'The edge of an enormous jungle, so dark green that it looked almost black, ran straight along the blue sea, which was covered by a fine mist. The sun was strong, the land seemed to shine with steam. Here and there we could see a flag flying beside a few huts which marked a tiny village, perhaps centuries old but still looking no bigger than the head of a pin against the jungle behind it. Every day the coast looked the same, but we continued to leave men at places – trading places – with odd, theatrical names like Gran' Bassam and Little Popo.

'I felt alone among these passengers and the crew. I had nothing to do on the boat and no point of contact with the men around me. The dull, lazy sea and the dark, unchanging coast seemed to keep me away from the truth of things. Was I living a lie? The voice of the water as it reached the shore was a positive pleasure, like the speech of a brother. It was something natural, something that had a reason and a meaning. A boat appearing from the shore also gave me an occasional contact with reality. The black natives shouted and sang as they worked, and although their faces looked unreal to me, they had a wild energy that was as natural and true as the sea along their coast. They were a comfort to me, but the feeling of reality they gave me did not last long.

'This comfortable feeling was easily frightened away. Once we saw a French battleship sitting near the shore and firing its long guns at empty earth, sky and water. The French crew were firing into a continent. There was a touch of madness to the exercise, even the sense of a joke; this impression was not lessened when someone on our boat told me very seriously that there was a camp of natives – he called them enemies! – hidden out of sight somewhere.

'We continued along the coast, stopping at more villages where death and trade existed in an atmosphere as quiet and airless as a hot cave. The dangerous waves seemed to warn us to stay away; death ran in and out of rivers, which were thick with mud, rotten plants and old roots, twisting and turning in powerless despair. The contents of nightmares surrounded us on all sides.

'It was more than thirty days before I saw the mouth of the River Congo, and my work and my boat were still more than three hundred kilometres further up the river. So as soon as possible, I began the next part of my journey to a post fifty kilometres higher up the river, from where I would begin the part of my trip on land.

'To get to the next post, I joined another steamboat and made friends with her captain, a thin, young, blond Swede who was permanently depressed. As we left port, he pointed at the shore with disgust and asked, "Have you been living there?" I told him I had, and he continued, "Those government gentlemen are a fine bunch, aren't they?" He spoke English both correctly and bitterly. "It's funny what some people will do for a few pennies. I often wonder what happens to that kind of man when he goes up the river." I said that I expected to find out. "Well, don't be too sure.

I took a man up a few days ago, another Swede, and he hanged himself on the journey."

"'Hanged himself! For what reason?" I cried.

"'Who knows? Perhaps the sun was too much for him, or maybe the country."

'At last we turned a bend in the river and saw houses on a hill and larger wooden buildings in a separate area. Here was pitiless sunlight, noise, dirt, and black natives everywhere. "There's your Company's Outer Station," said the Swede, pointing to this scene from hell. "I will send your boxes up. Good luck."

'As I walked up the path, which curved round large rocks and decaying pieces of old machinery that reminded me of dead animals, I noticed a group of trees to the left. I thought I saw dark shapes move in that shady spot, but the path was steep and I had to concentrate on it.

'The sound of a whistle made me jump, and I saw the black people around me start to run. Then a heavy, dull explosion shook the ground, smoke came out of a place to my right on the hill, and that was all. They were building a railway, but the explosion did not seem part of that activity. In fact, it seemed to have no purpose at all.

'I turned my head at the sound of six black men struggling up the path behind me. They walked slowly because they were chained together, each with an iron collar round his neck; they walked with straight backs because they were balancing small baskets full of earth on their heads. I could see every bone in their bodies and every breath that moved in and out of their chests. Although they passed very close to me, their staring eyes did not see me; in their unhappy state they had no sense of what was happening around them. They were called criminals this time, instead of enemies, and they, too, were suffering because of decisions they could not understand and that had been made by foreigners.

'Behind these ghosts of men came another black man wearing a Company uniform and carrying a gun. He stood straighter and lifted his gun to his shoulder when he saw me, since he was accustomed to treating all white men as bosses. He met my look with a large, devilish smile, which seemed to label us partners. To him, I was part of the great cause that had created this station and its laws.

'I changed my mind and instead of going up, I turned to the left to go down, wanting to let the line of criminals get out of sight before I climbed the hill. You know I'm not usually so sensitive. I've seen the effects of violence, greed and hot desire, and reacted calmly, but I could not watch those chained creatures as they were driven up that hill by the hired representative of a company that I was now a part of. Was it a warning? For a moment I stood still in horror. Finally, I started down the hill towards the trees I had seen earlier.

'I avoided a large hole which had no obvious purpose. Perhaps it was simply designed to give the criminals work to do; I do not know. Then I almost fell into a channel beside the path and noticed that it was full of broken pipes, brought here by ship to improve the station but ignored and eventually thrown away.

'At last I arrived under the trees. I thought I'd wander around in the shade for a few moments, but as soon as I looked around, I realised I had stepped into the shadowy circle of a true hell. It was silent except for the sound of the river, and nothing moved.

'In the weak light, desperate black shapes lay on the ground or leaned against trees with every possible look of pain, fear and despair. I heard another explosion on the hill and felt the earth gently shake under my feet. The work was continuing. The work! And this was the place where some of the workers had escaped to die.

'It was clear that they were dying slowly. They were neither enemies nor criminals now; they were not even men, but simply black shadows of disease and sadness, lying desperate and confused in the grey light. The Company, following the rules they had made, had taken them legally from the villages along the coast, put them in unfamiliar surroundings, fed them strange food and made them work. When they became ill and inefficient, they crawled away to this awful place. These dying shapes were as free as air, and almost as thin.

'Enormous, empty eyes looked up at me from beside a tree trunk, and I felt in my pocket for a bit of bread from the Swede's ship. I held it out to the man – maybe just a boy, it was hard to tell. Thin fingers closed slowly on the bread and held it, but there was no other movement and he did not look at me.

'Near the same tree there were others who were no more than bunches of bones under black skin. They stared at nothing in a horrifying, exhausted manner. They created a picture of the effects of violent defeat in a terrible war. Unable to move, I watched one of these sad creatures crawl towards the river. He drank water out of his hand, then sat in the sunlight and let his head fall to his chest. I could not stay in that awful shade any longer and hurried out towards the station.

'I had to stop when I met a white man who totally surprised me. At first, I was not even certain if he was real. He was wonderfully clean and beautifully dressed, with a shirt as white as snow, a stylish woollen jacket, an expensive necktie, new-looking trousers and polished boots. No hat. Neat hair, brushed and oiled, under a green umbrella to protect him from the sun. He was amazing, and even had a pen behind his ear!

'I shook hands with this handsome figure and learned he was the Company's chief accountant, and that all the accounts were done at this station. He had come out of his office for a moment, he said, "to get a breath of fresh air". I only mention this wonderful creature to you because it was from him that I first heard the name Kurtz, the name of the man, as I've said, who is so important to my memories of that time. But I also respected the accountant with his neat clothes and hair. Surrounded by dirt, decay and ugliness, he still paid attention to his appearance. That takes strength of character.

'The accountant had already been at the station for three years and, later, I asked him how he managed to dress so well. He was slightly embarrassed, but admitted that he had taught a native woman to look after his things. I also admired the fact that he was equally neat and organised in his job; the Company's accounts were in excellent order. Everything else in the station was a mess – people, machinery, buildings. Black workers arrived and departed, a stream of goods from Europe was dropped into the depths of darkness, and in return the Company took away their prize: ivory.

'I spent ten days at the station, and it seemed like a lifetime. I lived in a hut in the yard, but to escape from the constant confusion around me, I sometimes went into the accountant's office. It was in a simple, rough, unfinished building, and it was as hot inside as out in the yard. I sat on the floor while the accountant, always perfectly dressed and clean, sat at a high desk and wrote and wrote. Sometimes he stood up for exercise. When a bed for a sick, probably dying, customs officer was placed in there before the man was sent back to Europe, the accountant was slightly annoyed. "The noise of this sick person," he said, "upsets my concentration. Without my full attention, it is difficult to avoid mistakes in this climate."

'One day he remarked, without lifting his head from his work, "Further up the river, you will certainly meet Mr. Kurtz." This was the first time I had heard the name and I asked who Kurtz was. "He is an extraordinary person, in charge of a very important trading post. He sends in more ivory than all the other agents together."

'We were interrupted by more noise than usual in the yard. A group of traders with their carriers and servants had arrived. The accountant walked to the window and, looking out at the confusion, said, "What a terrible noise! When you must do your work correctly, you begin to hate those natives. Hate them to death." He remained quiet for a moment and then went on, "When you see Mr Kurtz, tell him from me that everything here is very satisfactory. I don't like to write to him at that Central Station. I don't trust our messengers." He stared at me for a moment and then began again. "He will rise far, very far, in the Company. He will be an important person in the management very soon. The people above us, the Council in Europe, you know, they have big plans for him."

'He turned back to his work. The noise outside had stopped, and I moved towards the door. The sick man was still on his bed, unconscious and feverish; the accountant, concentrating on his books, was writing perfectly correct numbers; and twenty metres below the office I could see the group of trees that sheltered the dying workers.

◆

'The next morning, I finally left that station with sixty natives and began a 300-kilometre journey on foot to find my steamboat. There is not much to tell you about that trip, but I remember paths that spread through the empty land, through long grass, through trees, along streams, up and down stony hills. The land was on fire with heat, and there was nobody around – not one person, not a hut. The natives had left a long time ago.

'It is not surprising that there were no people around. If gangs of mysterious foreigners with guns arrived in England and began kidnapping people and making them work as slaves, every farm and village there would soon be empty too.

'Day after day the journey continued. I walked through a great silence with only the sound of sixty men marching behind me, each carrying a thirty-kilogram load. Camp, cook, sleep, pack up, march. Now and then we heard the sound of drums from a great distance; a strange sound, attractive, suggestive and wild – perhaps it was as full of meaning as the sound of bells in a Christian country.

'I had a white man with me, too. He was not a bad character, but rather too fat and with the annoying habit of fainting on the hot hillsides, kilometres away from shade or water. One time after he had fainted, I was holding my coat over his head like an umbrella, to protect him from the sun. When he finally opened his eyes, I asked, "Why did you decide to come to Africa?"

'"To make money, of course. What do you think?"

'He upset me even more by getting a fever. He had to be carried, and because he weighed more than 100 kilograms I had quite a few arguments with the carriers. Some of them even ran away because of him, taking their loads with them. One afternoon the carriers dropped him accidentally, and he began kicking and shouting, "Kill one of them! Teach them all a lesson." But, of course, the carriers had run off. I remembered the old doctor in Brussels and his interest in the mental changes to Europeans in Africa. I felt I was becoming scientifically interesting.

'On the fifteenth day of this part of my journey, I saw the River Congo again and dragged myself into the Central Station. It was surrounded by trees and bushes on three sides and a border of smelly mud along the fourth.

'My first impression, which did not change during my time there, was that the place was a mess, with no responsible management and little or no purpose. As I walked up to the buildings, a group of white men appeared. They came and had a long, lazy look at me and then walked away again. One of them, a fat, nervous type with a big black moustache, stayed and started questioning me. When he learned why I was there, he said that my steamboat was at the bottom of the river.

16

'"What? How? Why?" I demanded.

'"Oh, it's all right," the man said. "The manager himself was there when it went down. In fact, you must go and see him immediately. He's waiting for you."

'Now when I think about the steamboat at the bottom of the river, I wonder if someone wanted to stop me from moving on. But at that moment, the fact that my boat was under water was simply the next problem for me to solve. The manager and his men had started up the river in a hurry two days before, and in less than three hours they had hit some big stones and torn the bottom out of her. She sank near the south bank. For a moment, I wondered what I should do now that my boat was lost, but then I realised I had plenty to do. In fact, I spent the next few months getting my boat out of the water, moving her back to the station and making the necessary repairs on her for going up the river.

'My first interview with the manager was very strange. There was nothing extraordinary about his physical appearance or about his behaviour, although he did not invite me to sit down after my thirty-kilometre walk. But perhaps the blue of his eyes was unusually hard and cold, and maybe there was something curious about his smile. I can picture it clearly, but I cannot explain why it made me feel uncomfortable. His strange smile, which appeared at the end of each speech, made everything he said seem somehow mysterious.

'He had been a common trader in that part of the world since he was a very young man – and nothing more. His staff neither loved nor feared him. They did not even respect him, but they obeyed him. He made people feel nervous, and you cannot imagine what a powerful effect that had on his workers. He was not good at organising the station nor at encouraging the men to work. He had no education, and no intelligence. How had he risen to the position he was in? Perhaps because he was never ill. He had served three terms of three years, and his good health had become a type of power.

'One time there was a very bad tropical disease at the station, and almost every white man was hit by it. The manager stayed healthy and said, "Men who come out here should have no stomachs." Maybe there was nothing inside him.

'He began to speak as soon as he saw me. "You were on the road a long time," he said. "I couldn't wait, had to start without you. The stations further up the river needed men and supplies. They had been waiting a long time, and I needed to check on them. The situation was very serious, very serious."

'He paid no attention when I tried to explain how I had arrived at the Central Station. He ignored me and continued talking.

'"There were whispers that a very important station was in trouble, and its chief, Mr Kurtz, was ill. Of course, I hoped it was not true, but Mr Kurtz is ..."

'I felt exhausted and cross and did not want to hear any more about Mr Kurtz for the moment. "I heard about Kurtz on the coast," I said, interrupting him.

'"Ah, so they talk about him down there. He is the best agent I have, an extraordinary man, of very great importance to the Company. I am very, very worried about him. But, tell me, how long will it take to ..."

'I interrupted him again. I was very tired and hungry and still standing. "How can I tell?" I almost shouted. "I haven't even seen the boat yet. But no doubt it will take some months to repair her."

'"Some months," he said. "Well, let's say at least three months before you can start up the river. That ought to take care of the affair."

'I rushed out of his hut (he lived alone), thinking that he was a fool. But later I changed my mind about him when I remembered how he had accurately calculated the time needed for the "affair".

'The next day I went to work on finding my boat and getting her in working order again. I turned my back on the manager and his station, in an attempt at holding on to the kind of life I knew and valued. However, sometimes I looked around me – at the station and at the agents, walking round in the sunshine with nothing to do. They reminded me of people in a strange religious group. They whispered the word "ivory"; it sounded like a prayer, but one spoken by the dead. My God! I've never seen anything so unreal in my life.

'And outside, beyond the borders of the station, the silent jungle gave me the impression of something great, timeless, deathless – like evil or truth. It waited patiently for these strangers – these enemies – to be defeated and to leave with as little warning as they had arrived.

◆

'They were horrific months. Various things happened. One evening a grass hut full of supplies burst into flames so suddenly that I thought the devil himself was playing games with us. I was smoking my pipe quietly beside the bits and pieces of my steamboat and saw everybody running around like crazy men. The fat man with the black moustache ran down to the river carrying a tin bucket. He shouted, "Everybody is behaving wonderfully, wonderfully!" Then he filled his bucket with river water and ran back towards the fire. As he ran along, I noticed that there was a hole in the bottom of his bucket.

'I wandered up. There was no reason to hurry. The hut had burned quickly and now there was nothing left except some smoke and a few red coals. To one side, someone was beating a screaming native who they said had caused the fire. I saw the poor man a few days later, looking very sick, and soon after that he walked into the jungle again and did not return.

'As I approached the fire, I heard a few words of a conversation between the manager and another man: "Kurtz … take advantage of this unfortunate accident …" They stopped talking when I said good evening to them.

'"Did you ever see anything like it? It's unbelievable," the manager commented before walking away from the scene.

'The other man stayed beside me. He was a young agent, an educated gentleman with a pointed little beard and a long, curved nose. He was not friendly with the other agents, and for this reason they believed he was the manager's spy. I had hardly spoken to him before and was happy to have a chat.

'He invited me to his room in the main building of the station, where I saw that he had some native spears and knives on the walls, some rather expensive luggage and writing equipment, and, to my surprise, a whole candle for himself. At that time the manager was the only man allowed to have his own candle.

'His job was to make bricks, but after more than a year at the station he had not produced a single brick. He was waiting for something that he needed from Europe. So he was the same as all the other white men at the station – waiting and doing nothing – although the only thing that seemed to come to them was disease. When they were healthy they whispered about the other agents and planned how to get appointed to a trading station where they could obtain ivory and make lots of money. They plotted against each other and were jealous of anyone's success, but they did no work; they simply waited.

'I had no idea why this new agent wanted my company, but as we chatted I discovered that he wanted information from me. He asked about my reasons for being there and about my contacts in Brussels. He thought I was lying when I had nothing to tell him, and he soon became bored with me.

'But as I rose to leave, I noticed a small, interesting painting in oils on his wall. It showed a woman wearing a blindfold and carrying a lighted torch. The atmosphere of the painting was dark and threatening.

'I asked about the picture, and the agent said, "Mr Kurtz painted it in this station more than a year ago. He was waiting here for transport to his trading station."

20

'"Can you tell me, please," I asked, "who is this Mr Kurtz?"

'"He's the chief of the Inner Station, but he is much more than that. He is an ambassador of pity, and science, and progress, and much, much more. He is a special man. He understands our purpose in being here. Today he is chief of the best station; next year he will be assistant manager of the whole company in this area. And two years from now, who knows? Perhaps you do."

'"Why would I know?" I asked.

'"You are part of the new, moral gang of honour and strength. The same people who sent Kurtz also recommended you."

'"I think you've made a mistake about me," I said.

'"Don't say that," the agent objected. "I trust what I can see with my own eyes."

'I suddenly realised that my aunt's contacts in Belgium had produced an unexpected effect on this young man. I was close to laughing.

'"Do you read the Company's private files?" I asked.

'He looked frightened but did not say a word, and I enjoyed watching the fear on his face.

'"When Mr Kurtz is General Manager," I added cruelly, "you won't have that opportunity again."

'He blew out his candle suddenly, and we went outside. The station was still busy and excited because of the fire. I turned towards the river and walked more quickly when I heard the soft cries from the black man who had been accused of causing the fire, but the young agent touched my arm to stop me.

'"Please don't misunderstand me. You will see Mr Kurtz long before I have that pleasure. I don't want him to get a bad impression of me."

'I let him continue and examined him as he spoke. I thought: "If I tried, I could put my finger through him and would find nothing inside but a little loose dirt, perhaps." I began to realise why he was so upset. He had planned to become assistant

21

manager under the present man. Kurtz's presence worried both of them, and now he wanted me to understand every detail concerning his position.

'As he talked and talked, I rested my shoulders against the wreck of my boat and stopped listening to him. Instead, I smelled the mud and looked at the jungle and at the river as it rushed silently past me. What kind of men were we who had come here? Would this land and this river control us or would we control them? What was beyond the edge of the jungle? Something big, something that could neither talk nor hear. I had heard that Mr Kurtz was in there and had heard stories about him, but I could not picture him. He was still as unknown and mysterious to me as a man from Mars.

'However, I had an idea about Kurtz even then, and although I hate lies — somehow they seem connected to death — I allowed this young agent to believe the lies he had heard about me. I let him think I had powerful friends in Brussels and that I was an important person in the Company. I had an idea that by claiming this position I might be able to help Kurtz one day. But, I repeat, I had no clear idea of Kurtz at that time. He was just a word, a dream to me, but a dream that had captured and surprised me.'

♦

Marlow was silent for a few minutes, and then he tried to explain something about his own philosophy.

'It is impossible to define the most important features of one's life in a particular time period,' he began. 'I'm talking about the things that make it true and full of meaning, things that are not always obvious but which are extremely powerful and serious. It is impossible to communicate this to you. We live, as we dream: alone.'

He paused again, trying to arrange his ideas more clearly.

'Of course, you understand more than I did then. You understand me, who you know ...'

It was very dark now, and I could hardly see the other men. For a long time, sitting apart, Marlow had been no more than a voice to us. Everyone else was silent; maybe they were asleep, but I was awake and concentrating on Charlie Marlow's story. I was listening for a clue that would explain my feeling of alarm, perhaps fear, as Marlow's words reached me through the heavy night air.

Marlow began again. 'I did not correct the young agent's impression of me. I let him think that I had the support of powerful men. But what did I really have? Nothing! Nothing except the wreck of an old steamboat.

'"Every man needs to make a success of his life," the agent began explaining to me again. "We aren't here to sit around and stare at the moon. There are geniuses among us, but even Mr Kurtz needs the right tools and intelligent men around him. I was sent here to make bricks, but with what? Now I try to help the manager in his office. What else can I do?"

'I thought he could get me the rivets I needed to fix my boat. I knew that there were cases of rivets down the coast in the station yard on the hillside, but there was not one rivet in *this* station where they were needed. Messengers and carriers came and went several times a week. They brought cotton handkerchiefs and glass jewellery, but no rivets.

'The agent did not want to talk about my problems with rivets. He wanted to talk about his own concerns: his job, his success, Kurtz. Kurtz needed those rivets, too, but this agent did not understand Kurtz or his needs. His attitude changed, and he began to tell me a story about a hippopotamus.

'"There's an old hippopotamus that has the bad habit of coming out of the water at night and wandering around the station grounds. The white men used to come out and fire their guns at the creature, but they were wasting their bullets. That animal belonged here and some kind of magic protected him. But there is no special magic to protect the men who come here."

'He stood for a moment in the moonlight and suddenly said, "Good night" and marched away.

'I turned, almost with a kind of love, to my true friend, my twisted, ruined steamboat, and climbed on board. This boat had given me a chance to find out what I could do. I'm lazy, I do not like work, but I like what work teaches you about yourself. You discover your own reality – for yourself, not for others – and it is something that other people can never understand.

'I was surprised to find that I was not alone. One of the mechanics I had made friends with was waiting for me. After working hours he sometimes came over from his hut for a chat, and we talked about his six children (left in the charge of his sister when his wife died) and his birds, which he raised as a hobby. He was a good worker, an honest man and an interesting talker. I shook his hand and shouted, "We're going to get rivets!"

'He jumped to his feet and cried, "No! Rivets! Really?" He could not believe his ears.

'The two of us danced around like mad men, making a terrible noise, which probably woke up a few people in the station. When we stopped celebrating, a great wall of silence seemed to come out of the jungle, like a wave of trees and leaves and plants which could sweep us humans away and out of existence. Then we heard the sound of ancient animals, but we turned our backs on the jungle and looked at each other.

'"We deserve rivets!" said the mechanic boldly.

'"They'll arrive in three weeks," I said, very confidently.

'But they did not arrive. Instead of rivets, a new disease arrived in the next three weeks: five groups of men from the Eldorado Exploring Company. Each group was led by a proud white man in new clothes, followed by his crowd of natives carrying every piece of equipment and type of supply that you can imagine.

'I believe the white agents had sworn to keep their company's business secret, but they talked like a gang of common thieves;

they seemed cruel without courage, greedy without a sense of adventure, and wild without strength. They had no ideas, no philosophy, no moral purpose; their goal was to steal a fortune from this land, without considering what they were destroying. I wondered whose money was behind this business, but I soon discovered that the uncle of our station manager was the leader of the five groups which crowded into the station.

'Physically he looked like a short, fat butcher from a poor neighbourhood, with clever, narrow eyes. During the whole time his gangs stayed in the station, he spoke to no one except his nephew. You could see the two of them wandering about all day with their heads close together in secret conversation.

'I stopped worrying about rivets. They were not worth the headaches. Without them I had plenty of time to think, and sometimes I wondered about Kurtz, although I was not very interested in him – not yet. But I was curious to see if this man, who had come out to the Congo armed with some sort of moral ideas, would climb to the top, and what he would do if he succeeded.

Chapter 2   Journey up the River Congo

'One evening, when I was lying peacefully on the deck of my steamboat, I heard voices approaching and soon recognised that they belonged to the manager of the Central Station and his uncle. I relaxed and was almost asleep when the two stopped near the boat, very close to my head, and continued to talk. I did not move – I was very sleepy – and bits of their conversation began to float up to me.

'"I'm as innocent as a little child, but I don't like to be given orders. Am I the manager or not? I was ordered to send him there. It's unbelievable."

"'It *is* unpleasant," agreed the uncle.

"'He asked the bosses in Brussels to send him there. He wanted to show them what he could do, so I was instructed to send him there," the nephew repeated. "His kind of power is dangerous."

'Their conversation continued and I could not hear everything clearly, but eventually they came close to me again and I heard the uncle say, "The climate might solve the problem for you. Is he alone there?"

"'Yes," answered the manager. "More than a year ago he sent his assistant down the river with a note for me. In it he told me to get the poor devil out of the country. He said he preferred to work alone instead of with any of the fools I sent him. I was shocked. He should not be allowed to speak to me in that manner."

"'Have you had anything from him since then?" asked the uncle.

"'Ivory," whispered the manager. "Lots of it – top quality. It annoys me. He makes more money for the Company than any other agent."

'Then silence. They had been talking about Kurtz. I was completely awake now and kept very still and quiet. I wanted to hear every word.

"'How did all that ivory reach this station?" asked the rather angry uncle.

"'He sent it in several boats with his clerk, a half-native, half-European. It appears that he started the journey himself with the clerk because his station needed supplies, but after 500 kilometres he changed his mind and returned to the station alone. What kind of man would leave a native in charge of all that ivory?"

'The manager and his uncle could not understand Kurtz, who they referred to only as "that man", but I began to get a clearer picture of him. I could imagine him in a boat with four natives taking him back into the jungle, to his empty and lonely station. Why did he turn back? Perhaps he was simply a good worker, but the clerk had, I also learned, reported that his boss had been very ill and was still not completely recovered.

26

'I could hear bits of the conversation below me again: "Army station − doctor − 300 kilometres − alone now − long delays − nine months − no news − strange stories."

'They came closer to me and I heard the manager say, "Perhaps it's one of those wandering traders. They watch for their opportunity and seize ivory from the natives."

'I wondered who they were talking about. It seemed to be someone in Kurtz's district.

'"We should hang one of them as an example. They are thieves, not competitors," said the manager.

'"Certainly," agreed the uncle. "Have him hanged! Why not? Anything − *anything* − can be done in this country." This suggestion surprised me, and I raised my head and watched the two men from my dark corner.

'"And remember, *your* position is not in danger," continued the uncle. "And why? The climate agrees with you − so you live; others give up and die. The danger for you is not here, it is in Europe, but I made arrangements before I left …"

'"The delays are not my fault," interrupted the nephew. "I did everything possible."

'"Very sad," agreed the uncle.

'"And his high ideas …" continued the manager. "He thinks each station should be a light to guide the natives towards better things, a centre for trade of course, but also a centre for improving, for educating. Can you imagine! What a fool! And he wants to be manager! No, it's crazy!"

'After a pause, the uncle asked, "Have you been well since you came out this time?"

'"Me? Of course. Absolutely fine. But the agents − oh, you wouldn't believe it. All sick. They die so quickly, too. I often don't even have time to send them out of the country."

'"Well, remember, your good health will protect you from all this," the uncle said as he pointed at the land − the jungle, the mud, the river – which hid death, evil, and a deep darkness at its heart. This surprised me and, without thinking, I jumped to my feet and looked at the edge of the jungle, in a hopeless search for some sort of answer there.

'I think they heard me, but they ignored me and walked back towards the station.

◆

'My weeks and months repairing the steamboat finally came to an end, and I started up the River Congo to Kurtz's station. My trip up that river was like travelling back to the beginning of the world, when plant life covered the earth and the big trees were kings. The air was warm, thick and heavy, and the sunshine brought us no joy. The wide stretches of water ran through islands covered in trees; it is as easy to get lost on that river as in a desert, and you feel completely separated from everything that is familiar. Sometimes, especially when I was very busy, a moment from the past appeared in front of my eyes. How did that dream suddenly come to me in this world of plants, water and silence?

'The silence was not peaceful. It gave me the sense of a great force, waiting to destroy us. But I had too much to do to worry about it. I had to worry about the physical dangers in the river: hidden banks, underwater stones, dead wood, unexpected changes in the water itself. Luckily the other danger – the hidden truth – was forgotten for a time. But I still felt it; I often felt that the silence was watching me and laughing at my silly tricks, as it watches each of you when you're doing your little jobs – for what? A few silver coins?'

'Don't be rude, Marlow,' a voice said, and I knew there was at least one other man listening as well as me.

'Forgive me. You do your jobs well, and I did not do badly either, since I managed not to sink that steamboat on my first trip. Imagine a blindfolded man trying to drive a van over a bad

28

road, and you'll get an idea of me, a seaman, trying to guide my steamboat through that dangerous river. You never forget the alarm you feel when the bottom of the boat hits something underneath it on the riverbed. It is like a blow to the heart. You wake up in the middle of the night and go hot and cold with the memory of it.

'I admit that the steamer did not float all the time. More than once, twenty of the cannibals on board had to get into the shallow water and push it along. The cannibals were part of our crew; they worked hard and behaved well. At least, they did not eat any human flesh while they worked for me. They had brought a supply of hippopotamus meat with them, which they ate even after it had gone rotten. Its smell brought the mystery of the jungle into my nose. When I think about it, I can still remember that horrible smell.

'In addition to the cannibals, and the other natives, I had on board the manager and three or four of the ambitious agents from the Central Station. Sometimes we saw a small trading station close to the riverbank, and when they heard the noise of our boat, the white men rushed out of their huts and welcomed us with joy and surprise. I got the impression that a type of magic held them there, and the magic word was "ivory".

'We continued our journey further into the silence, past millions of enormous trees which formed walls on both sides of the river. At the foot of these monsters, we crawled along like a tiny insect crossing the floor of a grand palace. It made you feel very small, very lost, but not totally depressed. Because, even if you were a small insect, at least you crawled forwards, which was exactly what you wanted to do. I thought about the agents and bet they were dreaming of how to make their fortunes.

'For me the little insect crawled towards Kurtz; my only purpose was to meet him. When the boat gave us trouble, we crawled very slowly and the trees seemed to close behind us. Perhaps they were making sure that we did not escape.

'We entered deeper and deeper into the heart of darkness; it was very quiet there, but sometimes at night we heard the sound of drums coming from behind the curtain of trees. The noise, which might mean war, peace or prayer, seemed to hang over our heads until the sun came up. Dawn was announced by a cold silence; the crew were asleep and our fire burned low; any sound made you jump. We were explorers on an unknown planet; we imagined ourselves as the first men in this new world, and we had to work and suffer to conquer it.

'But sometimes, as we struggled round a bend, we suddenly saw a grass wall or roof, then we heard shouts, hands clapping and feet stamping, and we saw black arms and legs moving under the heavy plant life.

'The steamer moved slowly past this excitement. These men from another age, from an ancient group of people – were they cursing us, praying to us, welcoming us? How could we know? They lived in an earlier, savage age, one that we had left behind and had forgotten; we floated past, secretly feeling shocked, like normal men watching the activities of men in a madhouse.

'We are accustomed to the idea of a conquered monster, one that is in chains or kept in a cage. But we were looking at something that was both monstrous and free. Like wild animals, these *men* shouted, jumped and spun, and made horrible faces at us. However, it was exciting to realise, but hard to accept, that they were human. They were our relatives, perhaps from our distant past, but part of the same family – our family. Ugly. Yes, it was ugly, but if you were brave enough, you had to admit that there was something deep inside you that responded to the noise and activities of these wild creatures.

'You began to suspect that there was a meaning in all of it which you understood. And why not? The mind of man is clever enough for anything, because everything is in his brain – all the past and all the future, too. Perhaps we were seeing the truth in a clear light, without the clouds of time covering it.

'A real man, an honest man, had to look at these savages without turning away. He had to meet their truth with his own truth and strength. Principles? Principles would not help him. Money, clothes, pretty objects – these things disappear at the first attack. No, a man needs a conscious belief.

'Are you wondering about *me* now? Are you asking yourself why I – with my concern for good and evil – did not land and join the natives in their song and dance? Well, no, I did not, and do you know why? Because I had no time. I had to watch the steam pipes and keep them working. I had to guide our old steamboat past dangers in front of us and underneath us. Our everyday reality was enough to save me from joining the savages.

'I was also responsible for looking after the native who was my fireman. He was a relatively educated savage; he could keep a fire going to create our steam. A few months of training had made him good at his job, but he was still a savage at heart. His teeth ended in sharp points and his hair was shaved into odd patterns; he had interesting marks on each of his cheeks and a piece of bone, as big as a watch, was stuck through his lower lip. But instead of shouting and dancing on the riverbank, he was hard at work at his place beside the fire. My fireman was extremely useful to me because he had learned the ways of steamboats. He fed the fire like a man honouring an angry god, and he worked efficiently and with energy to keep his god happy.

'We slipped past the natives and their noise and faced more kilometres of silence; we moved closer to Kurtz. But the water was dangerous and shallow, the roots of enormous trees were threatening, and the engine seemed to have an angry devil inside it. Neither the fireman nor I had time to examine our thoughts and fears.

◆

'When we were about eighty kilometres below the Inner Station and Mr Kurtz, we were surprised to see a grass hut, and beside it there was an old piece of flag on a pole and a neat pile of wood. We approached the bank, and on the woodpile we found a message written on a piece of board: "Wood for you. Hurry. Approach cautiously." There was a signature which we could not read, but it was not Kurtz – it was a much longer name.

'Hurry? Where? Up the river? Approach cautiously? Something was wrong further up the river, but we had no clues about what it could be.

'On shore I entered the hut and could see that a white man had lived there recently. There was a simple table, a pile of rubbish in one corner, and near the door I found a book. Its covers were missing and the pages were dirty with use, but the back had been lovingly sewn together with clean white cotton.

'It was an amazing discovery. Its title was *An Enquiry into some Problems for Seamen*, by a man named Towson – a captain in the King's navy. The book was over sixty years old and looked like dull reading, but I handled it carefully because it was obviously of great value to someone. As I looked at Towson's words, I forgot about the jungle and the agents and felt connected to something practical and real. The book was a wonderful surprise, but even more amazing were the notes in pencil that the owner had written down the side of each page. I could not believe my eyes! Imagine a man carrying a book about sailing into the jungle and studying it. It was an extraordinary mystery.

'My thoughts were interrupted by shouting from the steamer. The manager and the agents had moved the pile of wood onto the boat and were ready to depart. I quickly hid the book in my pocket and left feeling that I was being torn away from shelter offered by an old, dear friend.

'As we started up the river again, the manager said, "I suppose it was the hut used by one of those independent, wandering traders."

'"I think the man in the hut was English," I replied.

'"That fact will not keep him out of trouble if he is not careful," the manager warned.

'"No man is safe from trouble in this world," I added innocently.

'The water moved past us more rapidly now, and the steamer struggled against it. I found myself listening to every sound that came from below, expecting the poor boat to die at any moment. But still we crawled on. The manager appeared completely calm and relaxed while I worried and argued with myself about whether or not I would speak openly with Kurtz. But then, in a flash, I realised that neither my speech nor my silence would change anything for anyone. Did it matter what anyone noticed or ignored? Did it matter who was manager? The important parts of this affair, including the aims of both the Company and the main players, lay deep under the surface, beyond my reach, and beyond my power to change.

'Towards the evening of the second day we calculated that we were about twelve kilometres from Kurtz's station. I wanted to continue, but the manager told me that the river became more dangerous up there; we would be wise, especially because the sun was already low in the sky, to wait where we were until the next morning. In addition, he reminded me to remember the sign: "Approach cautiously". To be cautious, we must approach in the daylight, not in the dark.

'Sensible advice. I knew that twelve kilometres meant another three-hour journey, and I could see that the river was clearly becoming more dangerous. However, I was annoyed by the delay, although I knew that one more night would not matter much after so many months.

'We put our anchor down in the middle of the stream long before the sun had set. The trees made high walls on either side on this narrow part of the water, and we sat there, not moving and hearing nothing. You looked round, amazed, and wondered if you had gone deaf – then the night came suddenly and you thought you'd gone blind, too. At about three o'clock in the morning an animal – perhaps a large fish – hit the water, and the noise, like gunfire, made me jump.

'When the sun rose we were sitting in a thick, warm, white fog that limited our sight more than the night had. It did not move; it was simply there, surrounding us like something solid.

'At about nine o'clock, the fog lifted like a theatre curtain, and we had a quick view of the tall army of trees, and the thick jungle with the little red ball of the sun hanging over it. Nothing moved and then the curtain fell and again we were lost in white fog. But the silence did not last. Noises that we could not explain shook us and filled our ears. The hair stood up on the back of my neck. Were the screams coming from the fog itself? The noise ended with a burst of horrible cries which stopped suddenly, leaving all of us confused and frightened.

'"Good God! What is the meaning of this?" whispered one of the agents at my elbow. Two others rushed onto the deck with their guns, ready for action.

'The only thing we could see beyond the steamboat was about a metre of misty water around us – and that was all. The rest of the world was gone, had disappeared – swept away without leaving a whisper or a shadow behind.

'"Will they attack us?" a nervous voice asked.

'"They will butcher us in this fog," whispered another.

'The white men were shocked, almost offended, by this mysterious danger. The natives, on the other hand, seemed interested in the situation, quietly observing what was happening. The blacks' headman, a strong, handsome youth with a threatening look, stood near me.

'"Well, this is interesting," I said in order to sound friendly.

'"Catch them!" the headman shouted, opening his eyes wide

and showing a flash of sharp teeth. "Give them to us."

'"What would *you* do with them?" I asked.

'"Eat them!" he shouted, as he tried to see beyond the fog.

'This suggestion did not horrify me, because I remembered that this man and his friends were probably extremely hungry, especially since there had been no hippopotamus meat for more than a month. They had been hired for six months, but none of them had a clear idea of time. They belonged to an age without clocks or timetables. And, of course, no one had worried about food for them, and their dead hippo could not last six months – although it would have lasted longer if a certain quantity of it had not been thrown into the river during a quarrel with the agents. I did not blame the agents. No one could breathe the smell of rotten hippo meat while sleeping, eating and working for weeks, and not go crazy.

'The cannibals were receiving a kind of wage for their work: every three weeks they each received three fifteen-centimetre pieces of metal wire. The theory was that they could trade this "money" for anything they needed at the riverside villages. You can guess how that worked. There were either no villages or the people were unfriendly, or the manager, who ate food out of tins like the rest of us, did not want to stop the steamer for some useless business. I admit this *generous* salary was paid regularly by the Company, but I did not see any advantage in receiving it unless they made a meal of the wire itself, or used it to make hooks for catching fish.

'After the hippopotamus was gone, I saw the cannibals eating a strange mixture of some type of flour and water, which they kept in leaves. They swallowed small, dirty-looking lumps of this stuff from time to time, but it was so little food that I did not know how they stayed alive.

'Of course the question is, why didn't they eat *us*? They were suffering from terrible hunger, and there were thirty of them and five of us. They were big, powerful, courageous men, and they had no moral argument against eating human flesh, but something prevented them from having one of us for supper. What stopped them? Did we disgust them or were we unhealthy-looking? We were all thin by then and maybe even a little feverish. Or were they controlled by some kind of savage honour? But surely principles are ignored in the face of painful hunger. However, they did not eat us, and the questions remained – almost as hard to understand as the mysterious screams we had heard coming from behind the blanket of fog.

'The agents and the manager were still quarrelling about what to do next.

'"Turn to the left, into the bank," whispered one of the agents.

'"No, to the right," advised another.

'"It is very serious," said the manager's voice behind me. "I would be filled with despair if anything happened to Mr Kurtz before we reached him."

'I looked at him and saw that he seemed completely sincere. He was the kind of man who always wanted to appear to have the right feelings and to follow the correct course of action.

'"Shouldn't we move on immediately?" he asked, but we both knew that this was impossible. If we pulled up our anchor, we would be floating in air – in space – with no control over our direction. Even if we hit a bank, we would not know which bank it was or in which direction we were facing. We would crash into something and drown speedily.

'"I refuse to take any risks," I told him.

'"Well, you are the captain," he began politely, "and I must accept that you are the best judge in this situation."

'I turned away from the manager and stared into the fog. How long would it last? Our situation seemed hopeless. The approach to this genius Kurtz, out there somewhere in the cruel jungle searching for ivory, was full of more dangers than a beautiful princess had to face in a children's story.

'"Do you think they will attack?" whispered the manager.

'In my opinion there were several obvious reasons why they would *not* attack. First, the fog was thick, and they would get lost in it as easily as we would. Anyway, when the fog had lifted for a few short minutes, I had not seen any boats or canoes. If we stayed where we were, I did not think they could reach us.

'But, more than anything else, I did not think the natives would attack because of the sound of their cries. They were not frightening, war-like sounds; instead, they gave the impression of sorrow. Perhaps the sight of the steamboat had filled them with sadness. Maybe their extreme despair would turn into violence, but I did not think this was how they would react. I was certain that they would not attack us.

'The agents decided that I had gone mad. They wanted action, but I stood and watched the fog, although my eyes were of no use to me. The fog had buried us deep in a warm white cloud.

◆

'In the end the agents got the action that they wanted. We were not attacking or defending anything in the usual sense; our attack was caused by the force of our despair, and in reality it was purely for protection. It was about two hours after the fog lifted, and we were about three kilometres from Kurtz's station. We had just struggled to make our way round a bend when I saw a tiny island, no more than a bright green hill, in the middle of the stream. As we approached, I saw that the little hill was connected to a chain of shallow sandy areas under the water and stretched down the middle of the river like a man's backbone. I had to decide whether to go to the right or left of this stretch of shallow water, and since I knew Kurtz's station was on the west side, I guided the steamer along the western channel.

'As we entered the channel, I realised that it was much narrower than I had supposed. We had the string of shallow sandy areas to our left and to the right a high, steep bank covered in thick bushes. Above the bushes we could see row after row of enormous trees; many of their branches hung over the stream. It was late afternoon and there were already long shadows falling across the water, slowing us down and making us cautious and depressed. I kept the boat near the shore where the water was deepest.

'There were two little houses on the deck of our steamboat with open doors and windows, and these contained the fire and the machinery; a light roof covered the two small buildings. The boat's wheel was in a third little house, the pilot-house. I spent my days sitting on the front of the roof, and at night I tried to sleep on an old sofa beside the wheel in the pilot-house. I was on the deck, watching my pole, which showed me the depth of the water. One of the cannibals was beside me. Another native, also a strong, young black man who the previous captain had trained, was at the wheel. This pilot was good at his job when he knew I was watching him, but if he could not see me, his mind wandered and the boat ruled him.

'Without warning I saw the cannibal beside me suddenly fall to the floor and lie stretched out there. At the same time the fireman, who I could see below me, sat down beside the engine and covered his head with his arms. I was amazed. I had to keep my eyes on the river but noticed that there were little sticks flying at me; they were racing past my nose, dropping below me, hitting the pilot-house. All this time the river, the shore, the jungle, were perfectly quiet. The only noise came from the steamer. Then I understood: arrows! We were being shot at! I could see the pilot, that fool, lifting his knees high, stamping his feet and completely forgetting about the wheel, as we floated within three metres of the bank.

'I leaned right out to get the wheel and saw a face level with mine, looking straight into my eyes; and then, suddenly, I could see arms, legs, chests and staring eyes – the bushes were alive with black human bodies. The arrows flew out of the bushes, and I shouted at the pilot: "Turn the wheel! Get her going straight again!" He was frightened to death, but he followed my orders.

'There was total confusion on deck, and a voice screamed, "Can you turn back?" I was worrying about keeping the boat moving, when the sound of gunshots made me jump. The agents were firing bullets into the bushes while the arrows continued to rain down on us. Perhaps they contained poison, but they looked fairly harmless to me.

'Then screams and cries began to come from the bushes, and our black workers answered with their own shouts. I looked over my shoulder and saw that the pilot was not at the wheel, and the pilot-house was full of smoke. I shouted for the pilot and seized the wheel, but there was no room to turn, so I guided the steamer into the bank, where I knew the water was deep.

'The steamer struggled along slowly, pushing against low trees, broken branches, and flying leaves. I jumped out of the path of something that flew into one window of the pilot-house, past my head, and out of the other window. I could see the pilot, who had found a gun, shouting at the shore and waving the gun around, and I could see what he was looking at: shadowy forms of men running, jumping and floating through the bushes.

'Then something much bigger than an arrow appeared in the air, and the pilot's gun fell into the water. The man himself stepped back quickly, looked at me over his shoulder and fell on my feet. The side of his head hit the wheel twice, and the end of a spear, which he seemed to be holding at his chest, knocked over his little chair.

'The air was clear now and, looking ahead, I could see that in another hundred metres we could turn away from the bank; but my feet felt so warm and wet that I looked down at them. The pilot had rolled on to his back and stared straight up at me;

both of his hands held the spear, and now I could see that it had gone through his chest. My shoes were full of his blood and a dark red pool of it lay under the wheel. The agents' gunfire began again, and the pilot looked at me anxiously, but he still held the spear. His attitude suggested that it was prized by him, and that he feared I would take it from him.

'I turned away from the bleeding man and his spear to concentrate on the wheel. With one hand I felt above my head for the steam-whistle and hurried to pull it, sending out screech after screech. The angry, warlike noise on the bank stopped immediately and was succeeded by sad cries of fear and despair – sounds men make when the last hope disappears from the earth. The arrows stopped coming, and I could hear men running in the bushes – then silence.

'At that moment, one of the agents appeared at the door of the pilot-house. "The manager has sent me ..." he began in an official voice, but stopped when he saw the wounded pilot. "Good God!" he said, staring at the spear and the pool of blood.

'The agent and I stood over the pilot and watched him die without saying a word or moving his hands from the spear in his chest. In his final minute, he appeared to hear or see something we could not; then he turned his lips down and died with a sad, serious expression on his face.

'"Can you take the wheel?" I asked the agent at my side. He looked doubtful, but I seized his arm, and he knew he had no choice in the matter. To tell you the truth, I was very anxious to change my shoes and socks, as you can imagine.

'"He is dead," whispered the agent.

'"No doubt about it," I agreed as I pulled at my shoes. "I suppose Mr Kurtz is dead as well by this time."

'For the moment that was the only thing I could think about. Was my only purpose in travelling all this way to talk to a ghost? I felt disgusted with myself and threw one of my shoes into the river. I had always imagined Kurtz talking, not doing. I did not say to myself, "Now I will never see him," or "Now I will never shake his hand." I said, "Now I will never hear him." Kurtz was a voice. Of course I did connect the man with some sort of action. I had heard the stories, told by jealous and admiring men, of how he collected, traded or stole more ivory than all the other agents together. That was not the point.

'The point was that he was a genius, and that the most important of his gifts, the one that carried the real sense of the man, was his ability to talk. His talent with words: confusing, informing, the grandest, the most shameful, a stream of light, or thick, heavy darkness from the heart.

'I threw my other shoe into the river. I thought, "My God, it's finished. We are too late; he has disappeared – the gift has disappeared, killed by a spear or arrow. I will never hear that genius speak." My sorrow seemed to match the terrible sorrow I had heard from the natives in the jungle. I felt a despair that comes when your belief is destroyed or when you miss a perfect opportunity in life.

'Did one of you laugh? Do you think I'm crazy? Can't a man ever … Give me some tobacco for my pipe.'

There was a deep, silent pause, and then a match was lit, and Marlow's face appeared. He looked exhausted and his eyes were sad and tired; for a minute or two he concentrated on smoking his pipe.

'Crazy!' he cried then. 'This is the most difficult part of trying to tell my story. Here are the four of you, each with a good home – a butcher round one corner, a policeman round another, plenty of good food to eat, good weather. Everything normal from the beginning to the end of every year. And you say: "Crazy! Crazy!" What can you expect from a man who was so nervous, so frightened that he threw a pair of new shoes into the river?

'When I think about it now, I am amazed that I did not sit

down and cry. I felt destroyed by the idea that I would not have the honour of listening to the genius Kurtz. Of course I was wrong. That honour was waiting for me.

'In the end, I heard more than enough. And I was right, too. Kurtz was not much more than a voice. And I heard – him – it – this voice – other voices – all of them were not much more than voices. The memory of that time stays with me; it is alive, like the dying heartbeat of a long, disconnected conversation – silly, dirty, wild or simply cruel, without any kind of sense. Voices, voices – even the girl herself, his Intended – now ...'

He was silent for a long time.

'I finally conquered the ghost of his gifts with a lie,' he began again suddenly. 'Girl! What? Did I mention a girl? But she is not really part of this story. She is out of it – completely. They – the women, I mean – are out of it – and they should be out of it. We must help them to stay in their own beautiful world so that our world does not become worse. *She* had to be out of it. It was very strange to hear Mr Kurtz – who was still alive – speaking about "my Intended". You would have understood immediately that she was out of it.

'But to see Mr Kurtz – which I finally did – and his powerful head! The land had touched that head and now it was like a ball – an ivory ball. He was a completely different man from the one he had been in Europe. The Congo had taken him, loved him, got into his blood, eaten his flesh, and claimed his soul through some kind of mysterious native ceremony. He was the spoiled, favourite son, and he had accepted his new role enthusiastically.

'And ivory? You would not believe it. There were mountains of it around Kurtz's station. The old mud huts were bursting with it. It was easy to imagine that there was no ivory left either above or below ground in the whole country. We filled the steamer with it, and had to pile a lot on the deck. At least this way, Kurtz could see and enjoy it as long as possible.

'He referred to it as, "my ivory". I heard that many times, and, "my Intended, my ivory, my station, my river, my …" Everything belonged to him! I held my breath when he made such announcements; surely either the jungle or the river would laugh at his extraordinary claims.

'Everything belonged to Kurtz – but that was nothing. The big question was: What did *he* belong to? How many powers of darkness claimed him as one of theirs? It was not healthy to imagine who, or what, he had joined forces with. He had taken his place beside the devils of the land, and believe me, I am not talking poetically – I am perfectly serious.

'You do not understand what I'm talking about, do you? How could you? You have solid pavement under your feet. You're surrounded by kind neighbours who are always watching and are happy to share in your successes or your failures. Imagine living like Kurtz – alone, with no butcher or policeman, and in silence, without a neighbour warning you about public opinion and whispering about your affairs behind your back. These little things make a great difference to how we run our lives.

'When normal day-to-day routines disappear, you have to be faithful to yourself, trust yourself and depend on your own strength. Of course you may be a fool, someone too stupid to try a different path through life, too dull to notice that the powers of darkness are attacking you from every side. Fools are not clever enough to make a bargain with the devil for their souls.

'On the other hand, you might be a perfectly good person, someone who is deaf and blind to anything that is evil, and familiar only with people and ideas that are pure. In that case, the earth is only a stopping place on your journey towards a better, heavenly home. I cannot judge whether this is a better or worse way to live. But most of us do not exist in either of these two extremes. The earth for us is a place to live in, where we must accept earthly sights, sounds and smells. We breathe dead hippo, for example, and it does not harm us.

'There – in everyday life – don't you see? That is where you find your strength of character. You have to trust in your own ability, commit yourself to your business – even if the goals are unclear – and do your job. And that is difficult.

'Believe me, I am not trying to excuse or even explain what happened out there. But I am trying to explain Mr Kurtz – or the ghost of Mr Kurtz – to myself. This genius, this god or king of a completely foreign land, trusted me with his story before he disappeared completely. This was because he could speak English to me. Kurtz – before Africa – had been educated partly in England, and – as he said – he was sympathetic to the English way of life. His mother was half-English, and his father was half-French, and the rest of him was from all over Europe.

'With this background, you can see why the International Society for the Control of Savage Customs had hired him to write a report for them, to guide their future activities on the African continent. I've seen it and read it; it was well-written and meaningful, but perhaps a little theatrical. Seventeen pages of it – how had he found the time for such an exercise? But this must have been before his – how shall I say it? Before his nerves went wrong. That is how the Company described the situation – his nerves had gone wrong – but I am certain that there was nothing wrong with his nerves. I think he saw an opportunity to control his own fortunes and to rule his own world – something that very few men ever see. He began to join in, and even direct, certain midnight dances and savage ceremonies, which I eventually understood were done to honour Kurtz himself. Do you understand? He no longer worked for the Company; he was master of his universe.

'But Kurtz's report was a beautiful piece of writing, although after learning more about him, I could see how it held clues to his mental state and to his actions. In it he argued that we white people, because of our high level of development, "must appear to the savages as some type of god, and we come into their world with the power of gods." He continued by saying, "We were given unlimited opportunities to use our power for good." From that point in his report, his language and ideas seemed to fly, and I was carried along by his words. I found myself agreeing with everything he wrote; his opinions and his logic were brilliant. He gave me the idea of an extraordinary foreign Spirit which was ruled by a sort of grand Goodness. The power of his words made me come alive. He made me enthusiastic about the possibilities in life.

'Unfortunately, Mr Kurtz did not interrupt the magic power of his words with any practical suggestions on what actions to take, although there was a note at the bottom of the final page – something he had added at a much later date when his hand was shaky and his thinking was less clear. After the original seventeen pages, which were an honourable, almost religious report on the people around him, Kurtz had added a simple message which flashed like lightning across a calm blue sky and shocked the reader. It said simply: "Exterminate all the savages!"

'It was curious that Kurtz appeared to have forgotten this extra, added note, because later, when he was more or less his normal self, he encouraged me to read his report and to take good care of it; he believed it would help him in his career.

'I had full information about the report and about Kurtz's goals, and, besides, I was made responsible for Kurtz's memory. I've earned the right to forget Kurtz, to throw his story in the rubbish, among a pile of other dead ideas. But, you see, I cannot choose. He will not be forgotten. Whatever he was, he was not ordinary. He had the power both to charm and to frighten ordinary souls into magical dances and ceremonies in his honour; he could fill the minds of agents with doubts and fears; he had at least one true friend, and he had conquered one admirer in the world who wanted nothing from him.

'No, I definitely cannot forget Kurtz, although I am not sure it was worth losing a life to reach him. I missed my pilot – I missed him while his dead body was still lying in the pilot-house. Perhaps you will think my regret for a poor, uneducated black savage is strange. But don't you understand? He worked for me, he guided the steamer; for months he stood beside me – a help – an instrument. We were partners in a way. He piloted for me – I looked after him; I worried about him and tried to teach him. There was a connection between us that I became conscious of only after it was broken. And the depth of his final look remains to this day in my memory; that one moment cemented our relationship for all time.

'Poor fool! Why did he find that gun and try to join the battle? He had no self-control – just like Kurtz – like a tree that is easily blown from side to side by the wind. As soon as I had put on a pair of dry shoes, I pulled the spear out of his chest – I admit that I had my eyes tightly shut for that job – and then I dragged him out of the pilot-house. His heels knocked together as I pulled him over the little doorstep; his shoulders were pressed to my chest; I held him tightly from behind. And he was heavy! Heavier than any man on earth, in my opinion. Then without hesitating, and without ceremony, I pushed him over the edge of the boat. The river picked him up and carried him away like a blade of grass, and I saw the body roll over twice before I lost sight of it for ever.

'The agents and the manager were standing on the deck near the pilot-house, talking excitedly like a bunch of noisy birds. They were shocked at how quickly I got rid of the body. Perhaps they wanted to keep it for a funeral. But I also heard another, darker whisper spreading round the lower deck. There had been talk among the cannibals of making a meal of the dead body, but I had decided that if my late pilot was going to be eaten, it would be by the fishes.

'Now I took the wheel again, and going slowly, keeping to

the middle of the stream, I relaxed a bit and listened to the talk around me. They were certain that Kurtz was dead and the station had been burned to the ground.

'"Well, we punished them for killing Kurtz," one of the agents was saying. "We probably murdered an enormous number of them in those bushes. What do you think?" He was almost dancing with excitement at the thought of killing so many savages. He forgot that he had almost fainted at the sight of the pilot with a spear in his chest.

'"You made a lot of smoke," I commented innocently. Their shots had gone too high; they had hit bushes and trees, not bodies. You cannot hit anything unless you aim carefully and fire from the shoulder; but these fools fired with their guns at their waist and with their eyes shut.

'"The natives were frightened away," I continued, "when they heard the screech of the steam-whistle."

'My comment made them forget about Kurtz and raise a noisy protest at this attack, as they saw it, on their skills with guns, and perhaps on their honour.

'The manager ignored them and stood beside me at the wheel. "We must progress as far as possible before dark," he whispered urgently. As he said this, I saw something in the distance on the riverside; it looked like the shapes of buildings.

'The manager clapped his hands in surprise and cried, "The station!"

◆

'I edged the steamer towards the bank, still going slowly. Through my telescope I could see a hill with a few trees, but the ground had been completely cleared of the usual plants and bushes. The ruin of a long building sat on the top of the hill and was half buried in the high grass, and I could see large holes in its roof; the jungle and woods made a background for it. There was no fence of any kind, but a row of thin posts showed that there had been one previously; each post was decorated with a sort of round ball on top. Now the jungle was taking over again.

'The riverbank was clear, and I saw a white man in a large hat waiting there, waving to us energetically. I thought, in fact I was almost certain, that I could see human forms moving in the jungle behind him. I stopped the engines and heard the man on the bank instructing us to land.

'"We have been attacked," screamed the manager.

'"I know – I know. It's all right," shouted the other man cheerfully. "Come over here. It's all right. I'm glad to see you."

'His clothes and hat reminded me of something amusing I had seen somewhere. As I guided the steamer to the shore, I was asking myself, "What does this person look like?" Then suddenly I knew. He looked like a clown. His clothes were covered with bright squares of cloth: blue, red, yellow. He had pieces of material sewn on the back, on the front, on his elbows, on his knees. He had red borders on his jacket and at the bottom of his trousers; and the sunshine made him look extremely cheerful and wonderfully neat because you could see how skilfully his clothing had been made. He had a smiling, boyish face with fair skin, blue eyes and no beard or moustache.

'"Be careful, captain!" he shouted to me. "A large branch fell in there last night."

'I swore shamefully, not liking the idea of doing any damage to the bottom of my boat.

'The clown on the bank turned his little nose up to me and, all smiles, asked, "Are you English?"

'"Are you?" I shouted from the wheel.

'His smile disappeared, and he shook his head sadly. He seemed sorry to disappoint me.

'"Are we in time?" I asked.

'"He is up there," he replied, pointing up the hill. His face was like the autumn sky, cloudy one moment and sunny the next.

'When the manager and the agents, all of them carrying their guns, left the steamer and went to the house, this young clown came on board.

'"I don't like this situation," I said, "with these natives hiding in the bushes."

'"Nothing to worry about," he guaranteed me. "They are simple people," he added. "I'm very glad you have arrived. It has taken all my time and energy to keep them away."

'"But you said there was nothing to worry about," I cried.

'"Oh, they meant no harm," he said, but corrected himself when he saw the look of surprise on my face. "Well, not exactly, anyway." Then very cheerfully, he continued, "Look at this! Your pilot-house needs a good cleaning!"

'In the next breath his conversation was serious again, and he advised me to keep my fires going so that there was always plenty of steam. "Then you can blow your whistle if there's trouble. One loud screech will frighten them more than all your guns. They are simple people," he repeated.

'The clown continued to talk very quickly. I imagine that there were few opportunities for chatting, and now he was enjoying his first conversation in months.

'"Don't you talk to Mr Kurtz?" I asked.

'"You don't talk to that man – you listen to him," he said with admiration in his voice. "But now ..." He waved his arm and seemed to fall into a mood of despair and sadness. But in a moment he jumped up and began to talk quickly: "Brother seaman ... honour ... pleasure ... delighted ... introduce myself ... Russian ... son of a priest ... You've got tobacco! Excellent English tobacco! Now, you are a true brother. Do I smoke? Where can you find a sailor that does not smoke?"

'The pipe calmed him down, and gradually I learned that he had run away from school and had gone to sea in a Russian ship. Then he ran away again and served some time on English ships. He had made peace with his father, the priest, and was happy about that but added, "When you're young you have to see things, gather experience, fill your mind with new ideas, new knowledge."

"'Here!?" I interrupted.

"'You never know. I met Mr Kurtz here," he said, with the seriousness of youth.

'I kept quiet after that and listened to his story. "I found a Dutch trading-house on the coast and persuaded them to give me supplies and tools to get started. Of course I headed for the centre of this country with no more idea of what would happen than a baby would have. I wandered around the river for almost two years alone, cut off from everybody and everything. I'm not as young as I look – I'm twenty-five.

"'I met Van Shuyten, an old Dutch trader, and he often laughed and told me to go to the devil, but I stayed close to him, and talked and talked. Finally he got tired of listening to me, so he gave me some cheap things and a few guns and told me he hoped he would not see me again. Good old Dutchman, Van Shuyten. I sent him a small load of ivory a year ago, so that he can't call me a thief if I see him again. I hope he got it. Did you see my old house? I left a pile of wood there for you."

'I gave him Towson's book, the one I had found in his house, and he was so happy he almost kissed me.

"'It's the only book I had left," he said. "I thought I had lost it for ever. So many accidents happen to a man when he's travelling alone, you know. Canoes turn over sometimes – and sometimes you have to move away quickly when people get angry with you." He looked lovingly at his book.

"'You made notes in Russian?" I asked. "I didn't recognise the language when I saw it."

'He laughed, then became serious again. "I had a lot of trouble keeping these people off," he said, waving his arms at the jungle.

50

'"Did they want to kill you?" I asked.

'"Oh, no!" he cried, and then stopped.

'"Why did they attack us?" I wanted to know.

'He hesitated, then said, slightly nervously, "They don't want Kurtz to go."

'"Don't they?" I asked, curious to understand the situation.

'He gave me a look which was both mysterious and wise. "I tell you," he cried, "this man has educated me. He has made me see things clearly." He opened his arms wide and stared at me with his perfectly round little blue eyes.'

Chapter 3   The Mystery of Life Itself

I looked at this young Russian in his brightly coloured clothes and was amazed. There he was in front of me, looking like an actor who had just escaped from the theatre and was still wearing his stage dress. There he was – enthusiastic, brilliant. Why did a creature like that exist in this place? How had he stayed alive and succeeded? Why didn't he go home or just disappear? He could not be explained; he was a problem that could not be solved.

'"I went a little further," he said, as he started his strange story again, "and then even further, until I had gone so far that I don't know how I'll ever get back. Never mind. Plenty of time. I can manage. You take Kurtz away quickly – quickly."

'The beauty of youth protected him in some way. It made his poverty, his loneliness, and his despair at wandering aimlessly around this country acceptable – at least to himself. For months, for years, his life had not been worth a handful of pennies, but there he was, alive without a care, strong and full of hope, only because he was so young.

'I looked at him and admired him; perhaps I even envied him. Beauty pushed him on and kept him safe. He wanted nothing from this jungle except space to breathe in and permission to continue his great adventure. He wanted to face the greatest possible risks with the most danger to himself. He was totally ruled by a pure, uncalculated, impractical spirit. A clear flame, which had burned out any selfish thought, led him on, and maybe this is what I envied.

'I did not envy his extreme loyalty to Kurtz, though. He had not thought about it logically. This commitment came to him, and he accepted it eagerly. To me, this blind loyalty appeared the greatest danger this young Russian had had to face.

'He and Kurtz had come together unexpectedly, like two ships at anchor beside each other. I suppose Kurtz wanted an audience, because the Russian told me about a time when the two were camped together in a forest.

'"We talked all night, about everything," the youth reported excitedly. "I forgot about sleep. The night did not seem to last an hour. Everything! Everything! Of love, too!"

'"Ah, he talked to you of love!" I said, finding his conversation very amusing.

'"It isn't what you think," he cried, almost in tears. "It was about love in general. He made me see things – all sorts of things."

'He threw his arms up and looked at the sky. I looked around at the scene we found ourselves in, and I do not know why, but I guarantee you that this land, this river, this jungle, the curve of this brilliant sky had never appeared so hopeless and so dark to me, so beyond human thought, so unsympathetic to human weakness.

'"And have you been with Mr Kurtz since that night?" I asked.

'The Russian had, as he informed me proudly, nursed Kurtz through two illnesses – a rather dangerous job, it seemed – but usually Kurtz wandered alone, going deep into the jungle.

'"Often when I came here – to this station – I had to wait days and days before he returned, but he was worth waiting for

– sometimes," the youth began again.

"'What was he doing?" I asked. "Was he exploring or looking for something special?"

"'Of course," the Russian said, "he discovered a lot of villages, and a lake, too. I'm not sure where that was – it was dangerous to ask too many questions. But most of his trips were to search for ivory."

"'But the manager said that Kurtz hadn't had any goods to trade for a long time," I argued. "He wasn't a trader any longer, was he? He was a thief. To speak plainly, he stole from this country. But did he work alone?"

'The youth said something about the villages around the lake, but I could not understand him.

"'Kurtz persuaded those natives to follow him, didn't he?" I suggested.

'The Russian seemed nervous, but he said proudly, "They loved him." I could see that this young man understood this emotion because he loved Kurtz, too.

"'What can you expect?" he cried. "He came to them with thunder and lightning, you know – and they had never seen anything like it. It was terrible. Mr Kurtz could be very frightening. But you can't judge him as you would judge an ordinary man. No, no, no! For example, one day he wanted to shoot me, but I don't criticise him for that."

"'Shoot you? What for?" I shouted.

"'Well, I had a small quantity of ivory that the chief of the village near my house gave me because I had helped him and his people by shooting small animals for them. Kurtz wanted that ivory and nothing I said persuaded him that he had no right to it. He told me to give him the ivory and leave the area or he would shoot me. That was the kind of thing he could do, and no one ever tried to stop him. He could have any ivory he wanted, and he could kill anyone he wanted to. So I had no choice – I gave him the ivory. It didn't really matter to me, but I didn't leave the area – I couldn't leave him. I just stayed out of his sight for a short time, until we were friendly again.

'"Then he had his second illness, and after that I had to stay away from him again, but I didn't mind. He was living most of the time in those villages on the lake. He came down to the river occasionally, and sometimes he wanted to see me and talk to me, but sometimes it was better for me to be careful and stay away from him.

'"He suffered a lot and hated all this, but he couldn't give up and get out of here. When he was friendly to me, I begged him to leave while there was time; I offered to go back with him. He sometimes agreed to go, but then he went off on another ivory hunt – disappeared for weeks – lived among the natives – forgot what he had said, what he had promised."

'"He's mad, isn't he?" I said.

'"No, you've got it all wrong. If you could hear him talk, you would not dare to suggest such a thing."

'I looked through my telescope while we were talking and examined the shore, sweeping along the long house from side to side and from front to back. The idea that there were people in the bushes, so quiet – as quiet as the ruined house on the hill – made me nervous.

'Nature gave me no sign, no key to understanding the amazing story that I was putting together from what I was hearing. The jungle was unmoved, like the closed door of a prison, hiding its knowledge behind its forbidding silence.

'"Mr Kurtz came down to the river recently," the Russian explained. "He brought all the fighting men of the lake villages with him after spending several months up there with them."

'I pictured Kurtz in those villages acting like a king or a little god, and then perhaps coming down to the river again to find more ivory. I guess his greedy, worldly goals had become more important to him than his purer, possibly religious, goals.

However, according to the Russian, when Kurtz reached the river, he had suddenly become very ill.

'"I heard that he was lying in bed, unable to move or take care of himself, so I took the opportunity to come up here," he continued. "He was in a very bad state, very bad."

'I took up my telescope again and looked up the hill at the house. There were no signs of life, but I could clearly see the ruined roof, the long wall behind the tall grass, three little square windows, each one a different size from the others. And then I moved my eyes slightly away from the house and suddenly one of the fence posts came sharply into view. Do you remember what I told you about those posts? I had noticed that they were each decorated with a round ball on top, which surprised me in such a plain, discouraging place.

'But now I had a much closer view, and it caused me to jump back in horror. I went carefully from post to post with my telescope, and I saw my original mistake. The round balls were not there to decorate the posts – they had a different purpose, and they were not balls. They were human heads, and all except one of them was facing towards the house. I must admit that I was not as shocked as you may imagine – I jumped when I saw the heads because I was surprised, having expected to see wooden balls. Now I looked more carefully at the head turned in my direction – and there it was, black, dried, sunken, with closed eyes. It seemed to be asleep at the top of its post, and its dried-up lips showed a narrow white line of teeth which seemed to be smiling at a happy dream which would never end.

'Afterwards the manager reported that Mr Kurtz's methods had ruined the district for any further trade. I have no opinion on that point, but I want you clearly to understand that there was nothing profitable in having those heads there. They only showed that Mr Kurtz was out of control; his various needs and desires governed him, and his fine thoughts and his clever words had disappeared.

'I think this knowledge came to Kurtz at last – but only at the end. However, the jungle and the river had discovered his greedy secrets early and had punished him for his terrible attack on them. I think the land had whispered things to him about himself which he did not know, or which he could not understand until he was faced with this great loneliness – and the whisper charmed him and caught him in its magic. It filled his soul because he was completely hollow inside …

'The Russian was watching me as I examined the shore. He began to talk again when I put my telescope down, and the heads returned into the distance. "I didn't dare to remove the heads. I wasn't afraid of the natives; they only follow Mr Kurtz's orders. His power is extraordinary. The natives make camps around his house, and the chiefs come every day to see him. They crawl …"

'I stopped him. "I don't want to know anything about the ceremonies used to honour Mr Kurtz."

'I had a strange idea, a curious feeling that hearing the details of the honours received by Kurtz from the natives would be more offensive to me than seeing the human heads under his windows. I recognised the heads as an uncomplicated, savage practice with a right to exist, but Kurtz sitting as a god above these people horrified me.

'The Russian looked at me in surprise. I suppose he did not understand how anyone could have a different opinion of Kurtz from his own. He forgot that I had not heard any of Kurtz's rare speeches on love, justice, correct behaviour in life – or perhaps other serious topics. The Russian had honoured Kurtz as much as any of the savages had.

'"I don't know exactly why those men were killed," he swore. "But I'm sure these heads were the heads of rebels."

'"Rebels!" I shouted, not believing my ears. What word would I hear someone use next to describe the natives? I had heard "enemies", "criminals", "workers" – and these were rebels. Those heads looked very quiet and peace-loving to me on their sticks.

'"You don't understand how life in this country affects a man like Kurtz," cried that man's last loyal admirer.

'"But what about you?" I interrupted.

'"Me? I am a simple man. I have no great ideas. I don't want anything from anybody. You can't compare me to ..." He paused because his feelings were too strong for him. "I don't understand," he complained. "I've been doing my best to keep him alive, and that's enough. I was not involved in this. I have no abilities as a nurse, and there hasn't been any medicine or proper food here for months. It is shameful the way the Company has forgotten him and has given him no help lately. A man like this, with such important ideas. Shameful! Shameful! I – I – haven't slept for the last ten nights ..."

'His voice went quiet in the calm of the evening. The shadows of the trees grew longer and slipped down the hill, past the ruined house and the row of posts, while we talked. On the steamer, we were still in sunshine, and the river stretched beyond us, shining in the late sunlight. We could see no one on the shore, and the bushes were silent and unmoving.

◆

'Suddenly, round the corner of the house, a gang of black men appeared; they seemed to have come up from below the ground. They walked through grass that was as high as their waists, carrying a simple, rough bed. Without warning, a painful cry cut through the calm air like a sharp arrow flying straight to the heart of the land; from this scene from a nightmare, streams of human beings – with spears in their hands and no clothes on their bodies, with wild eyes and savage steps – poured into the clear space at the edge of the jungle. The bushes and the grass shook for a time, and then everything stood still and waited with silent attention.

'"We're dead if he doesn't say the right thing to them," the

Russian whispered. The small group of men with the bed had stopped, too, halfway to the steamer – also, it seemed, in terror. Kurtz, the man on the bed, sat up, thin and ill-looking, and raised his arm above his head.

'I leaned over and spoke to the Russian youth. "Let's hope that Mr Kurtz, who can talk so well about love in general, will find a good reason to spare us this time."

'I was greatly offended by the stupid danger of our situation. Why should we be terrorised by this madman? I could not hear what Kurtz was saying, but through my telescope I could see him pointing and giving commands, as he stared at the crowd of black men around him from ghostly eyes.

'Kurtz – Kurtz – that means *short* in German, doesn't it? Well, the name was as true, as honest as everything else in his life – and death. He looked more than two metres tall. His blanket had fallen off, and I could almost see his heart beating in his painfully thin chest. He looked like an ivory figure of death, waving his long arms at the silent black men surrounding him. He opened his mouth wide and created a black hole that threatened to swallow all the air, all the earth, all the men around him.

'The sound of his deep voice reached me weakly. I suppose he was shouting. Then he fell back on the bed suddenly and the bed shook as the men carried it forwards again, down to the steamer. At almost the same time, I noticed that the crowd of savages began to disappear into the jungle as suddenly and as quietly as they had appeared.

'The agents and the manager followed the bed, with some of the agents carrying Kurtz's guns. I imagined that these supplied the thunder and lightning that the great man used for making an impression on the savages. I watched the manager bend over the bed and speak to Kurtz as they moved towards me. Finally they laid him down in one of the little rooms on the boat where there was just enough space for his bed and a small chair. I could see that he had examined his private letters, which the manager had delivered to him, and his hand held a few of these. He had fire in his eyes but a relaxed look on his face. He did not appear exhausted by disease, nor did he seem troubled by pain. This ghost looked satisfied with himself and totally calm; it seemed that for the moment he was finished with emotions and feelings.

'He picked up one of the letters, and looking straight at me said, "I am glad." Those special recommendations from my aunt's friends had had an effect again. He spoke very few words, almost without moving his lips, and the voice amazed me. It was deep, strong, real – a voice that could command, from a man who looked like a ghost. However, he had enough strength and power to end us all if he wanted, as I shall explain.

'The manager appeared silently at the door. I stepped out of the room and closed the curtain behind me. I stood on the deck with the Russian and we both stared at the shore, while the agents watched us. We could see dark human figures in the distance, moving across the shadowy edge of the jungle, and near the river we saw two tall black men wearing war paint and leaning on their spears. At the same time, a wild, beautiful woman moved from right to left along the lighted shore. At first I wondered if she was real or another ghost.

'She walked proudly in careful, measured steps with handsome pieces of cloth and savage jewellery hanging beautifully from her neck, arms and shoulders. She held her head high; her hair was arranged in a complicated style, which reminded me of an ancient soldier's headpiece. She had metal plates protecting her legs to the knee and her arms to the elbow. A spot of red was painted on each cheek; a number of glass chains decorated her neck, and strange bits and pieces of stuff hung from her body and clothes and shone and shook with every step she took. Finally, she was also wearing a large quantity of ivory, the product of several elephants. She was savage, of course, but she was amazing, wild

59

and wonderful; there was something dark and threatening in her bold actions. In the silence that had fallen on the whole sorrowful land, all the energy, all the mysterious life of this place seemed to turn towards her; the land was faced with a picture of its own dark, wild soul.

'She came down to the water's edge, stood still and stared at us. Her face looked full of sorrow and silent pain, but I could also see a struggle going on inside her. Was she trying to make an important decision as she looked at us? A whole minute passed, and then she took a step forwards. Her clothes and jewellery danced lightly around her, and then her heart seemed to fail her and she stopped. The Russian gave a soft cry, and the agents whispered behind me. The woman suddenly opened her strong arms and threw them straight up above her head, appearing to have a powerful desire to touch the sky. A horrible silence hung over the scene.

'She turned away slowly, walked along the bank and passed into the bushes to the left. The last things we saw before she disappeared was her shining eyes.

'"If she had tried to come on board, I believe I would have tried to shoot her," said the Russian nervously. "I risked my life every day for the last fortnight to keep her out of his house. She got in one day and made a great noise about the pieces of cloth I was using to mend my trousers. Perhaps it was because I wasn't properly dressed at the time. Anyway, she shouted and argued with Kurtz for an hour, pointing at me now and then, but I don't understand her native language. Fortunately for me, Mr Kurtz was too ill to listen to her that day, or I would have been in trouble. It's all too much for me, but it's over now."

'At that moment I heard Kurtz's deep voice behind the curtain, where he was talking to the manager.

'"Don't pretend you came here to save me. You came here to save the ivory, you mean. Save *me*! I've had to save you, and now you are interrupting my plans. Sick! I'm not as sick as you want me to be. I'll achieve my goals – my ideas will remain alive – I will return and show you what can be done. You and your little ideas are annoying me. I will return ..."

'The manager came out. He honoured me by taking my arm and leading me to one side for a private chat.

'"We have done everything we can for him, haven't we? But we can't hide the fact that Mr Kurtz has done more harm than good to the Company. He did not understand that it was the wrong time for his type of forceful action. Cautiously, cautiously – that's my principle. We must still be cautious. This district is closed to us for a period of time. It's a disaster! Our trade will suffer, although there is a remarkable quantity of ivory here. We must save it, and somehow we will, but look at how dangerous our position is – and why? Because Kurtz's method was faulty."

'"Do you," I said, looking at the shore, "describe it as a *faulty method*?"

'"Without doubt," he stated confidently. "Don't you?"

'"No method at all," I said quietly after a few seconds.

'"Exactly!" he shouted, happy that I seemed to be agreeing with him. "I knew something like this was going to happen. It shows a complete lack of judgement. It is my duty to point it out to the proper offices."

'"Oh," said I, "your assistant – the brick-maker – what's his name? I bet he'll be able to write a good report for you."

'He appeared confused for a moment. It seemed to me that the air around me had become evil, almost diseased, and I found myself turning towards Kurtz in my mind, for comfort from this terrible atmosphere.

'"From what you have said, I believe Mr Kurtz is a remarkable man," I said without hesitation.

'I had surprised him and he gave me a cold look, and then said quietly, "He *was*," and turned his back on me and walked away.

'That ended my partnership with the manager; I now found myself paired with Kurtz as an enemy of the Company and a defender of faulty methods. Now *I* was faulty! But, at least now I could choose my own nightmare.

'I had not actually turned towards Kurtz, who was almost dead already, but towards the land, the jungle, the river. And for a moment it seemed to me that I was buried in an enormous grave full of horrifying secrets. I felt a terrible weight on my chest, smelled the wet earth, sensed the presence of an unseen evil, felt trapped in a night that would never end.

'I jumped when the Russian tapped me on the shoulder and tried to tell me something. "Brother sailor," he began, "there are too many secrets. I have knowledge of matters that would damage Mr Kurtz's good name."

'I waited. For this young man, Kurtz was obviously not dead; in fact, to him Kurtz was a god and still very powerful. "Well," I said at last, "speak up. We are both Kurtz's friends – in a way."

'"You know, sir, that I would not speak freely to you if we were not both seamen. I know I can trust you, but I suspect that there is much bad feeling towards me from the other white men."

'"I believe you're correct about that," I said, remembering a conversation I had heard between the manager and one of the agents. "The manager thinks you ought to be hanged."

'"I should get away from here as quickly and quietly as possible," he said very seriously. "I can't help Kurtz any more, and the others would soon find an excuse for killing me. Who would stop them?"

'"Perhaps you *should* go, especially if you have any friends among the savages near here," I advised.

'"Plenty," he said. "They are simple people – and I don't need anything. I don't wish any harm on these whites here, but Mr Kurtz's good name is very important to me. And you, as a brother seaman, and ..."

'"Don't worry," said I after a time, "Kurtz's good name is safe with me." I had no idea how truly I spoke those words.

'"Listen," the Russian said, lowering his voice, "Kurtz ordered the attack on the steamer. He hated the idea of someone coming here and taking him away. I don't understand these matters. I am a simple man. But Kurtz thought it would frighten you away, that you would give up the search for him because you would think he was dead. I could not stop him, although I had an awful time trying to."

'"Well," I said, "he is all right now."

'"I suppose so," the Russian whispered, not sounding sure of this fact. '"But you'll keep our little secret, yes?" he asked anxiously. "It would be awful for Kurtz if anybody here ..."

'I promised to keep my eyes open and my mouth shut.

'"I have a canoe and three black natives waiting for me not very far away. Could you give me a few bullets for my gun? And maybe a little of your good English tobacco? Between seamen, you know?" Then at the door of the pilot-house he remembered one more request: "Do you possibly have a spare pair of shoes? Look." He raised his leg to show me shoes that were held together by pieces of string.

'I found him an old pair of shoes, which delighted him, and with those on his feet, his bullets in one pocket, his Towson in another, and tobacco and pipe in another, he seemed very happy to be returning to his wandering ways.

'"I'll never, never meet a man like him again. He read poems to me, even some that he had written. Poetry! Can you imagine, in a place like this?" the Russian said with great admiration. "Mr Kurtz opened my mind to all kinds of things. He changed my life!"

'"Goodbye," I said.

'He shook my hand and disappeared into the night. Sometimes I wonder if I really met him, or was he possibly another ghost?

◆

'I woke up soon after midnight and remembered all the warnings the Russian had given me. A sense of danger made me get up and have a look round. On the hill a big fire burned, lighting up a corner of the station-house. One of the agents was up there with a few of our black workers, carrying guns and guarding the ivory.

'Behind the house, deep within the jungle, I could see a circle of red fires in the darkness, which marked the exact position of the camp where Mr Kurtz's followers were keeping watch, waiting to see if he needed them. The steady sound of their drums and their voices filled the air as it came out of the jungle and had a calming effect on my half-awake senses. I believe I fell asleep standing on the deck, but awoke suddenly when I heard a burst of shouting from the natives which stopped as quickly as it had begun. I turned and looked into Kurtz's sickroom. A light was burning inside, but Mr Kurtz was not there.

'I think I would have shouted for someone if I had believed my eyes. But the shock frightened me, not because I was in danger, but because something painful, something beyond my ability to bear in my mind or soul, had been thrown at me without warning. Within seconds, these feelings had passed and I was faced with the possibility of real, physical danger: a battle, or even death. I welcomed this reality, and it calmed me so much that I forgot about shouting for help.

'There was an agent wrapped in a blanket and sleeping in a chair within a metre of me, but he had not woken up at the sound of the natives' shouting. I left him in his comfortable chair and jumped on the bank. I remained faithful to Mr Kurtz – it had been decided that I should stay faithful to him – it was written that I should be loyal to the nightmare of my choice. I was anxious to deal with this ghost alone, and to this day I do not know why I was so jealous of sharing this strange, dark experience with anyone.

'As soon as I got on the bank I noticed a broad path through the grass. I remember feeling quite excited when I said to myself,

"He can't walk – he is crawling on his hands and knees – I've got him now."

'The grass was wet, but I walked rapidly, ready for a fight. I think I had the crazy idea of jumping on him and giving him a good beating. The old Belgian woman knitting with the cat on her knees came into my head, and I thought she was not the best person to be waiting for me at the end of this affair. I imagined a row of agents firing bullets into the air, missing the mark as usual. I thought I would never return to the steamer and pictured myself living safe, but alone, in the jungle until I was a very old man. Silly ideas, you know. I even thought the beat of the drums was the beating of my heart, and I was pleased that it was so calm and regular.

'I kept on the path, and then stopped to listen. The night was a dark blue space, shining with drops of water and starlight, in which black creatures stood very still. I thought I could see something moving ahead of me, so with unusual courage, I left the path and ran in a wide circle. My plan, which I thought was very clever, was to get in front of any danger. I was circling in on Kurtz – two players in a kind of childhood game.

'I found him, and if he had not heard me coming, I would have tripped over him, but he stood up in time. He rose from the earth looking long, pale and unsteady. He stood silent like a ghost in front of me, while at my back the fires burned among the trees and many voices continued to come out of the jungle. My clever plan had worked, but when I faced him, I saw that I was in real danger. What would happen if he shouted for his followers to come and help him?

'"Go away – hide yourself," he said in his deep, strong voice. It was awful. I looked over my shoulder and saw that we were within thirty metres of the nearest fire. A black figure, maybe one of the chiefs, came towards us, waving his arms at me.

'"Do you know what you are doing?" I whispered to Kurtz.

"'Perfectly," he answered, raising his voice for that single word, making it sound both far away and loud. "If he wants to, he can start a big argument and then we will both be killed," I thought to myself.

"'You will be lost," I said. "Completely lost." By an amazing chance, this was the right thing to say at that moment. I knew he was already lost, but those words helped to create an atmosphere in which a friendship could begin – maybe something that could last until the end – even beyond.

"'I had enormous plans," he whispered weakly.

"'Yes," said I, "but if you try to shout I'll break your head open with …" There was not a stick or a stone near us. "I will silence you for ever," I corrected myself.

"'I was at the dawn of great things," he said in a voice full of sadness and regret, a voice that made my blood turn to ice. "And now this stupid manager arrives …"

"'Whatever happens, your success in Europe is guaranteed," I promised him. I did not want a physical struggle with him, and I would not have lasted very long with his followers so close. I had to break through the magic of the jungle, which seemed to attract him and awaken the savage side of his character. Only this, I believe, had driven him out to the jungle, towards the fires and the drums; only this had led him beyond the limits of rules and laws and had given him permission to follow a different path.

'Do you understand what I was afraid of? It was not the possibility of getting hit in the face or knocked on the head, although I admit I was afraid of that, too. I was frightened because I had to deal with this man, this creature who did not now accept the rules of God or man. He was not connected to this earth, and I, like the savages around him, had to pray to him – and to his own new, exaggerated, unimaginable inhumanity. There was nothing either above or below him, and I knew it. I cursed him! He had kicked the world I understood to pieces. Where did that leave me? Was I standing on the ground or floating in the air? How would I live through this night?

'I've been repeating the words we said – but what do they mean? They were common everyday words, the ones we use every morning when we wake up. But behind them, there was the suggestion, the whisper of words we hear in dreams, especially those in horrifying nightmares.

'Soul! I struggled with my soul more than any man before me. And I was not arguing with a madman because, believe it or not, his intelligence was perfectly clear. It was concentrated on himself, it is true, but because he could think clearly, I thought I had a chance of reasoning with him. There was no other way for me to escape – unless, of course, I killed him there and then, but with the natives so near, I was not going to try that.

'His intelligence was clear, but his *soul* was mad. After spending so much time alone, his soul had looked within itself and it had gone mad. I was witness to this madness; I heard his soul speak in his final rich burst of words and phrases, and it had the power to destroy one's belief in humanity.

'I struggled to understand Kurtz, but he struggled with himself, too. I saw it – I heard it. I watched him battle with a soul that knew no rules, no belief and no fear, but kept struggling blindly with itself.

'I surprised myself by staying relatively calm, and slowly guided him back down to the steamer with his bony arm round my neck. When he was stretched out on the bed again, I wiped my forehead and noticed that my legs were shaking, although he was not much heavier than a child.

◆

'When we left at midday on the next day, Kurtz's followers, who had remained behind the curtain of trees, flooded out of the jungle again, filled the shore and covered the hill with a crowd of breathing, shaking black bodies. I fired up my engine and turned downstream, with two thousand eyes following the action of this noisy, powerful river-god, beating the water with its terrible tail and breathing black smoke into the air.

'At the front of the crowd on the shore, three men covered in red mud from head to foot marched energetically along the beach. They stamped their feet and shook a bunch of black feathers and a dried animal skin as we passed. They shouted amazing things at us, sounds that had no connection to a human language; and the crowd behind them answered these voices with their own deep, practised cries.

'We had carried Kurtz into the pilot-house where there was more air. Lying on his bed, he stared through the open window. Suddenly the crowd separated, and the proud, beautiful woman that we had seen earlier rushed down to the edge of the stream. She stretched her hands towards us and shouted something. All the savages joined with her in a rapid, thundering song.

'"Do you understand this?" I asked Kurtz.

'He looked out past me with sadness and fire in his eyes; his expression was a combination of sadness and hate. He did not answer me immediately, but I saw a mysterious smile appear on his pale lips.

'"Do I not?" he said slowly, struggling for air; the words had seemed to be torn out of him by an unworldly power.

'I saw the agents on the deck preparing their guns, getting excited about shooting at the natives. To stop them, I pulled the string of the whistle. The savages stopped and looked at the sky in true terror.

'"What are you doing?" shouted the agents. "Don't frighten them away!"

'I pulled the string again and again. The savages ran, they jumped, they tried to hide, they did everything they could to escape from the horror of the whistle's screech. The three red dancers had fallen flat, face down on the shore, appearing dead. But the wild, beautiful woman did not react to the noise; like a tragic queen, she stretched out her strong arms, pointing after us over the sad and shining river.

'And then that stupid crowd on the deck started their sport, and the shore disappeared behind the smoke from their guns.

◆

'The brown stream ran rapidly out of the heart of darkness, taking us down towards the sea with twice the speed of our journey upwards; and Kurtz's life was running rapidly, too, pouring out of his heart into the sea of cruel time. The manager was very calm; he had no important worries now. He viewed both Kurtz and me with a certain degree of understanding and satisfaction: the "affair" had ended as he had wished. I saw the time approaching when I would be the only remaining member of the "faulty methods" group. The agents wanted nothing to do with me either; they considered me as one of the dead. It is strange how I accepted my unexpected partnership with Kurtz; his nightmare was forced on me when I saw the actions of these cruel, greedy conquerors in that dark land.

'And Kurtz spoke. A voice! A voice! It rang deep until his last breath. His body became weak but the voice remained strong and moving, expressing the empty darkness of his heart.

'And he struggled! He struggled! The wasteland of his exhausted brain was troubled by ghosts now – ghosts of wealth and fame which his talented voice could still talk about in the most expressive words and phrases. My Intended, my station, my career, my ideas – these were the subjects for his occasional clever speeches.

'The ghost of the original Kurtz visited the bedside of this false Kurtz, who was waiting to die. But both the devilish love and the unearthly hate that the man had discovered fought for his soul.

And what kind of soul was it? One that had been filled with savage emotions and had searched for fame, recognition and the appearance of success and power, while knowing that they were all false.

'Sometimes he was childish and hateful. He wanted kings to meet him when he returned to Europe; he wanted people to praise his success. "You show them you have something in you that is really profitable, and then there will be no limits to the recognition you receive for your abilities," he advised. "Of course, you must always start with the right goals – always."

'I listened to the moral twists and turns in his ideas as I guided the steamer through the twists and turns in the river.

'"Close the window," said Kurtz one day. "I can't bear to look at this any longer."

'I closed the window and then there was a long silence.

'Finally Kurtz spoke directly to the land: "I will break your heart before I am finished."

'We had trouble with the boat – as I had expected – and had to stop near an island to make repairs. This delay was the first thing that shook Kurtz's confidence. One morning he gave me a packet of papers and photographs, all tied together with a shoe-string.

'"Keep this for me," he said. "That unprincipled fool" – he meant the manager – "probably believes he has a right to look through my boxes when I am not looking."

'Later that afternoon I saw him again. He was lying on his back with closed eyes, but before I could leave quietly, I heard him say, "Live right, die, die …" I stopped and listened but there was nothing more. Was he practising a speech in his sleep, or was it a phrase from a newspaper story? He had been writing for the papers, and he told me that he intended to do so again, "to advertise my ideas. It's my duty."

'I could not break through his darkness. I looked at him as you stare down at a man lying at the bottom of a deep channel where the sun never shines. Unfortunately, I did not have much time to give him; I was making the necessary repairs on the steamer and living in a mess of engine parts, tools and rivets – things I hate, because I do not understand them very well. I worked long hours, until my legs felt too weak for me to stand.

'One evening I quietly went into the pilot-house and was surprised to hear Kurtz's shaky voice say, "I am lying here in the dark waiting for death."

'"That's nonsense!" I said, staring directly into his eyes, although I do not believe he knew that I was in the room.

'Kurtz was changing and that evening I had the opportunity to examine him closely. The change in him was something I had never seen before and hope I never see again. I was not affected by this new and different man, but I was very interested in him. It seemed that a screen had been moved away, and now for the first time I could see him clearly.

'And what did I see on that ivory face? The expression of dark pride, of cruel power, of cowardly terror – and of a hopeless despair – all of these things were written there. Was he living his life again and examining every detail of desire and surrender during those last moments when he saw things clearly? From time to time he cried in a whisper at a figure, a picture that only he could see. He repeated his cry, a cry that was no more than a breath of air …

'"The horror! The horror!"

'I closed his curtain, left the pilot-house and joined the agents at the dining table. I took my place opposite the manager, who lifted his eyes to give me a questioning look, which I successfully ignored. He relaxed comfortably in his chair, with that confident smile of his which expressed the depths of his cruelty. We ate in silence as a constant shower of flies surrounded the lamp, the tablecloth, and our hands and faces. Our meal was interrupted when the manager's servant boy suddenly put his black head round the door, and said in a voice full of hatred:

"'Mr Kurtz – he dead.'"

'All the agents, led by the manager, rushed out to look at the dead body. I remained at the table and continued eating a little of my dinner. I believe the others thought that I had no feelings, but they did not understand. There was a lamp on the table – light, do you understand? And outside it was so horribly, horribly dark.

'I did not look at the body; in fact, I did not go near the remarkable man who had pronounced a judgement on his own soul on earth. The voice was gone. What else had there been? But I know that the next day the agents buried something in a muddy hole.

'And then they tried to bury me.

'However, as you can see, I did not join Kurtz in his grave there and then. No, I did not. I remained on this earth to finish the dream, to find out how it ended, and to show my loyalty to Kurtz again.

'Life is funny – a mysterious arrangement of cruel logic for a useless purpose. The most you can hope to get out of life is some knowledge of yourself, but that usually comes too late, and you are left with a collection of regrets.

'I have struggled with death. It is the most unexciting battle you can imagine. The scene for the fight against death is a grey place, with no activity, no audience, no noise, and without honour, without the great desire for victory or the great fear of defeat. It is an unhealthy place with a sickly atmosphere in which you believe in neither your own right nor your enemy's right to win.

'But what do we expect during that all-important moment? Will the answers to great mysteries – to the mystery of life itself – be shown to us? I was within seconds, within centimetres of my end, my last opportunity to find some great knowledge, some understanding, and I found that nothing came to me. I had nothing to say.

'This is the reason why I swear that Kurtz was an extraordinary man. He had something to say, and he said it. I have been close to death; I have been in his position when he lay on his bed staring but not seeing. He could not see me or the wall or the curtain, but he could see the whole universe; he could see clearly into every heart that beat in the darkness. He made his judgement on the world: "The horror!"

'He was a remarkable man. His final word expressed some sort of belief; it had truth, it had power, it mixed desire and hate. It defined him as a rebel.

'Do you know, I cannot remember the terror or pain I felt when I was close to death. No! But I *can* remember Kurtz's journey to death. I experienced that much more than I experienced the approach to my own end. Of course, he took that final step; he really did go over the edge, while I was allowed to pull back from the edge and go on with life. Perhaps this is where the difference lies; perhaps you do not receive all the truth and wisdom that life has to offer until that final moment when you step into a world that is hidden from the living.

'Perhaps that is the way life works. I like to think that my final word would also have been wise and true, but nothing could match Kurtz's final cry. It was a confident statement, a moral victory that he had gained by facing many defeats, by standing up to horrifying terrors, and by taking his own cruel pleasures. But you cannot deny that it was a victory! And that is why I remained loyal to Kurtz until his death, and even beyond – even a long time after returning from Africa, when I heard another pure soul speaking with Kurtz's powerful, brilliant voice.

◆

'No, they did not bury me in Africa, but when I look back, there remains a period of time which I look at through a kind of fog, like taking a journey through a world that had no hope in it and no desire. I found myself back in Brussels disliking the sight of people hurrying through the streets, doing business with each other, seizing what they could, eating their awful food, drinking their unhealthy beer, dreaming their silly and meaningless dreams. They interrupted my thoughts. I judged them and was annoyed by their lives full of stupid importance, because I felt so sure that they could not possibly know the things I knew. They were ordinary and safe, and their everyday lives were offensive to me. I wondered if they knew anything that was important or true and had to stop myself from laughing in their faces, although I had no desire to talk to them or to teach them anything.

'Please understand that I was not very well at that time. My temperature was seldom normal in those days. I was unsteady on my feet and probably looked like a madman, staring and smiling bitterly at perfectly respectable people as I walked along the pavement. My dear aunt was trying to "nurse up my strength", but that was not what I needed. My imagination needed nursing, but she could not help me with that.

'There were various affairs that I had to settle, including deciding what to do with the bunch of papers given to me by Kurtz. I learned that his mother had died recently, cared for by his Intended, so I would not be delivering the packet of papers to her.

'Then a neat man with an official manner and wearing a pair of gold glasses visited me one day and began by making polite conversation. It soon became clear that he wanted Mr Kurtz's "documents". I was not surprised because I had had two arguments with the manager about these papers while I was still in Africa. His manner became threatening when he understood that I was not going to give him anything that had belonged to Kurtz.

'"The Company has the right to every piece of information about every area of its business. We believe that Mr Kurtz's knowledge of the unexplored regions near the River Congo was very broad and unusual for a white man – owing to his great abilities and to the difficult circumstances in which he found himself; therefore …"

'I guaranteed him that Mr Kurtz's knowledge, although it was extraordinary, did not consider the problems of trade or accounting.

'"I think you will agree that it would be a tragedy to lose any scientific information that Mr Kurtz collected," my visitor began again, listing more and more reasons for giving the Company all of Kurtz's papers.

'I offered him Kurtz's report on the Control of Savage Customs, after I had torn off the bottom where Kurtz had written his later note about exterminating the savages.

'The Company man accepted it eagerly, but after a quick look he turned to me and said in his official voice, "This is not what we had a right to expect."

'"Expect nothing else," I said. "There is nothing else except his private letters."

'"Well, if you are not willing to cooperate," my guest said, "I will leave, but I warn you that you will hear from the Company's lawyers soon." Then he left as quickly as possible.

'But he was not the last visitor who was curious about the bunch of papers. Two days later I was visited by an old gentleman, with dirty grey hair covering his shiny coat-collar, who introduced himself as Kurtz's cousin.

'"I want you to tell me everything about my dear cousin's final moments," the old man began.

'After I had given him a truthful, but uncomplicated report of Kurtz's death, he began to talk about his cousin. "Did you know that he was a great musician? If he had chosen music as his profession, he would have been a great success," said the man, who was also a musician, I believe.

'I did not doubt anything the man said, but even now I am unable to say what Kurtz's profession actually was, or whether he had one or not. I wonder which was the greatest of his talents: was he a painter who wrote for the newspapers, or a journalist who could paint? Even his cousin was not sure about the answer to that question, but we both agreed that he was a universal genius. He left happily with a handful of family letters and a few bits and pieces of art and jewellery that Kurtz had collected in Africa.

'The last visitor who came to me with questions about Kurtz was a journalist with a short, straight moustache, and an eye-glass on a broad string. He began by saying, "I am very anxious to know something about the death of my dear colleague."

'During his visit, he gave me another picture of Kurtz: "The man was a natural politician; he could excite people, persuade them of his way of thinking. Between you and me, he did not have a talent for writing, but he definitely could talk! When he spoke at a large meeting, you could feel the electricity moving through the crowd. He believed in ideas – do you understand? – and he could change ordinary people into believers. He would have been an extraordinary leader of a new, progressive political party."

'"What party?" I asked.

'"Any party," answered my visitor. "He was a rebel – an extremist. Didn't you see that in him?"

'"Yes, I think I understand what you mean," I agreed.

'After a second's pause, he continued, "Do you know what persuaded him to go to Africa in the first place?"

'"Yes," said I, and handed him Kurtz's famous report for the International Society for the Control of Savage Customs. "You can print this if you think there is an interest in this kind of thing."

'The journalist took a quick look at the report and left with it under his arm. Perhaps he was satisfied with this reward for his time.

'Now I was left with a thin packet of letters and a small painting of the Intended. My impression from the picture was that she was beautiful – I mean she had a beautiful expression. I know that artists can lie, and the sunlight lies, too, but I felt that no artificial tricks could hide the truthfulness in the girl's eyes. She seemed ready to listen without a thought for herself, without suspecting anything bad about the speaker. I decided that I would visit her and return the painting and those letters to her.

'Was I curious about her? Yes, but I also had another feeling about the situation. I had given away everything that had belonged to Kurtz: his soul, his body, his station, his plans, his ivory, his career. The only thing left was his memory and his Intended – and, in a way, I wanted to give those things away, too, and leave them in the past. I wanted to surrender my past with Kurtz, to bury it with him. I cannot explain or defend my actions; I'm not really certain about what I wanted. Perhaps it was a way of showing my unconscious loyalty to this man who had been so important to my life. I do not know. I cannot tell. But I went.

'I thought his memory was like the other memories of the dead that live in every man's life – a shadowy impression, left on the brain by dead friends and family as they leave this life. But when I reached the high, heavy door, between the tall houses on a quiet, respectable street, I suddenly had a clear picture of him on his sick bed, opening his mouth wide and creating a black hole that threatened to swallow all the air, all the earth, all the men around him. To me, at that moment, he was alive – not only him, but also his dark power and his persuasive voice.

'Kurtz, or his ghost, seemed to enter the house with me – the sick bed, his carriers, the noisy crowd of obedient followers, the heavy sadness of the jungle, the brilliance of the river, the beat of the drums – regular like the beating of a heart – the heart of a conquering darkness. It was a moment of victory for that wild land; it was rushing forwards to take control, and I would have to hold it back to protect and save another soul.

'Clear memories of Kurtz flooded my brain. I could see him where I had found him in the jungle, surrounded by the fires and the watchful eyes of his followers; I could hear his words and remembered how simple and terrible they were. He begged and he threatened; he expressed his most evil desires and the horrible despair in his soul.

'Later I could picture his relaxed manner, when he said one day, "All this ivory now is really mine. The Company did not pay for it. I collected it myself at a very great personal risk. But I am afraid that they will try to claim it as theirs. It's a difficult case. What do you think I ought to do? Should I oppose them? The only thing I want is justice."

'He wanted no more than justice – no more than justice.

'I rang the bell beside a large door on the first floor, and while I waited, Kurtz seemed to stare at me out of the shiny wood. His stare conquered and hated the whole universe. I seemed to hear the whispered cry, "The horror! The horror!"

'The sun had gone down, and I waited in a grand sitting room with three high windows from floor to ceiling. The heavy furniture, the shining piano, the cold white stone fireplace – everything in this fine room reminded me of funerals. A high door opened – closed. I rose.

'She came towards me, dressed all in black, with her pale head floating towards me in the soft light. It was more than a year since his death, more than a year since the news reached her; it seemed she would remember and cry for him for ever. She took both my hands in hers and whispered, "I had heard you were coming."

'I noticed that she was not very young – I mean she was not girlish. She was an adult and had a grown-up's ability and strength for loyalty, for belief, for suffering. The room seemed to have grown darker; all of the sad light from the cloudy evening seemed to have found a home in her hair and on her face; her dark eyes – innocent, deep, confident, trusting – looked out at me from a pale, pure cloud of light. She carried her sad head like someone who was proud of her sorrow; I expected her to say that she was the only person who knew how to honour him in death.

'But while we were still shaking hands, I saw a look of awful despair and sadness come on her face, and I understood that her emotions were not affected by time. For her, he had died only yesterday. This feeling was so strong that for me, too, he seemed to have died only the day before – no, just the minute before. I saw her and him in the same moment of time – his death and her sorrow. I saw her sorrow at the exact moment of his death.

'Do you understand? I saw them together – I heard them together. She said, with deep sadness in her voice, "I am still alive." My ears heard her despairing regret, and at the same time, I heard the whisper of Kurtz's endless, living attack on her. What did he blame her for? Did she have to live for ever with the belief that she had failed him?

'I asked myself what I was doing there; I felt a sense of alarm in my heart, like a person who has accidentally walked into a place full of cruel, nonsensical mysteries. I felt that these were mysteries that no human being should see.

'She pointed to a chair for me, and we both sat down. I laid the packet gently on the little table beside her, and she put her hand over it.

'"You knew him well," she whispered, after a moment of sad silence.

'"Close friendship develops quickly out there," I said. "I knew him as well as it is possible for one man to know another."

'"And you admired him," she added. "It was impossible to know him and not admire him, wasn't it?"

'"He was an extraordinary man," I said with little confidence. But she stared at me with such force, such emotion, and she watched my lips for more, so I went on, "It was impossible not to …"

'"Love him." She finished my sentence eagerly, leaving me surprised and unable to speak. "How true! How true!" she continued as I stared at her. "But no one knew him as well as I! He honoured me with all his trust. I knew him best."

"'You knew him best,'" I repeated. And perhaps she did. But with every word spoken the room was growing darker, and only her forehead, smooth and white, remained lit by the undying light of belief and love.

"'You were his friend,'" she went on. "His friend," she repeated, a little louder. "I know how important you were because he gave you this packet, and he sent you to me. I feel that I can speak to you — and I must speak. I want you — you who heard his last words — to know I have deserved him ... It is not pride ... Yes! I am proud to know I understood him better than anyone on earth — he told me so himself. And since his mother died I have had no one — no one — to — to ..."

'I listened. The darkness grew deeper. I was not even sure if Kurtz had given me the right packet. I suspected that he wanted me to take care of another bunch of his papers which, after his death, I saw the manager examining.

'And the girl talked and talked, finding comfort because she was sure I would listen sympathetically; she talked in the way that thirsty men drink. I had heard that her family did not want her to marry Kurtz; he was not rich enough perhaps. He had suggested to me that his relative poverty had driven him to Africa.

"'Anyone who heard him speak became his friend,'" the Intended continued. "He recognised what was best in people and made them see it. It is the gift of the great among us." Her voice was very low; I seemed to hear notes of mystery, despair and sorrow. They reminded me of the movement of the river, of the trees bending gently in the wind, of the whispers of wild crowds, of the weak sound of unclear words shouted from a distance, of a voice speaking from beyond the entrance to endless darkness. "But you have heard him! You know what I am talking about!" she cried.

'"Yes, I know," I said with despair in my heart, but agreeing with her because she was faithful to that great dream that shone in the darkness. I could not protect her from that victorious darkness; I could not even defend myself against it.

'"What a loss to me – to us!" she corrected herself generously; then she added in a whisper, "A great loss to the world." By the last light from outside the windows I could see her shining eyes, full of tears that would not fall.

'"I have been very happy – very fortunate – very proud," she went on. "Too fortunate. Too happy for a short time. And now I am unhappy for – for life."

'She stood up. Her pale hair seemed to catch all the remaining light in a flash of gold. I rose too.

'"And of all this," she continued sadly, "of all his promise, and of all his greatness, of his generous mind, of his honourable heart, nothing remains – nothing but a memory. You and I …"

'"We shall always remember him," I said quickly.

'"No!" she cried. "It is impossible that all this will be lost – that such a life is sacrificed and nothing except sorrow remains. You know what great plans he had. I knew of them too – perhaps I could not understand all of them, but others knew and understood. Something must remain. His words, at least, have not died."

'"His words will remain," I said.

'"And his example," she whispered to herself. "Men looked up to him – his goodness shone in every act. His example – I cannot believe that I shall never see him again, that nobody will see him again, never, never, never."

'She raised her arms and stretched them out towards an imaginary figure disappearing into the night. Never see him! I saw him clearly in that moment and shall see his powerful, persuasive ghost as long as I live. And I shall see her too, a tragic queen, who in that one movement reminded me of another beautiful queen, decorated with powerless jewellery, feathers, and ivory, tragically stretching her strong black arms over the river of darkness.

'She said suddenly in a very soft voice, "He died as he lived."

'"His end," I said, with dull anger rising in me, "in every way fitted his life."

'"And I was not with him," she whispered. My anger melted away, and I felt enormous pity for her.

'"Everything that could be done ..." I whispered.

'"But I believed in him more than anyone on earth – more than his own mother, more than himself. He needed me! Me! I would have prized every word, every look, every breath."

'I felt my heart turn cold. "Don't," I said.

'"Forgive me. I – I – have mourned so long in silence ... You were with him – to the end? I think of his loneliness. Nobody near to understand him as I would have understood ... no one to hear ..."

'"I heard his last words ..." I said, but I stopped, feeling frightened for her.

'"Repeat them," she said in her tragic voice. "I want something – something – to live with."

'I wanted to shout, "Don't you hear them?" The dark night was repeating them all around us, in a whisper that seemed to grow dangerously loud like a rising wind: "The horror! The horror!"

'"His last word," she repeated, "to live with. Don't you understand, I loved him – I loved him – I loved him!"

'I settled my thoughts and emotions and spoke slowly.

'"The last word he pronounced was – your name."

'I heard her take a short breath, and then my heart stood still, stopped by her terrible cry of victory, but also of pain.

'"I knew it – I was sure!"

'She knew. She was sure. I heard her crying; she had hidden her face in her hands. I thought the house would fall down around me before I could escape, but nothing happened. The heavens do not fall, the world does not come to an end for something so small.

'But would the heavens have fallen if I had given Kurtz the justice which he had earned? He had said he wanted justice. But I could not tell her the truth. It would have been too dark, too painful.'

◆

Marlow stopped and sat in silence. Nobody moved for a time.

'The tide has turned,' said the Director, suddenly, 'but we have lost our advantage.'

I raised my head. Our departure was blocked by a large bank of clouds, and the calm waterway leading to the ends of the earth ran sadly under a grey sky – seemed to lead into the heart of a great darkness.

ACTIVITIES

Chapter 1

Before you read

1 How many present-day African countries can you name? What were their names during the nineteenth-century colonial period? Which countries did they belong to?

2 Can you list both advantages and disadvantages for a nineteenth-century African country in being a colony of a powerful European country?

3 Explain why you think people have traditionally been attracted to sea voyages and unexplored lands.

4 Discuss the differences between a physical and a psychological journey. Which is more difficult or dangerous?

5 Look at the Word List at the back of the book. Which word on the right describes:

a	a piece of equipment?	*telescope*	*agent*
b	a loud sound?	*screech*	*crawl*
c	a violent act?	*knit*	*exterminate*
d	business	*trade*	*sacrifice*
e	something a boat builder needs?	*rivet*	*anchor*
f	something for a party game?	*blindfold*	*hippopotamus*
g	a well-loved person?	*monster*	*intended*
h	a condition without hope?	*savage*	*despair*

6 Choose five words from the Word List to use in a frightening story. Talk about your ideas for a story with a partner.

While you read

7 Write the name of the person or people being described.

a	He has the look of a poet or philosopher	....
b	They are not interested in running a country.	....
c	She has important contacts in Belgium.	....
d	He is Danish and is killed by a native.	....
e	This country owns the Congo.	....
f	He likes to measure men's heads.	....
g	He hangs himself after going up river.	....

h They are found under the trees at the
Outer Station. ....

i He is very clean and beautifully dressed. ....

j He sends in more ivory than any other agent. ....

k He makes people feel nervous. ....

l They wait, whispering *'ivory'*. ....

m They have their own candles. ....

n He is chief of the Inner Station. ....

o He is excited at Marlow's promise of rivets. ....

p He is the boss of the men from the
Eldorado Exploring Company. ....

After you read

8 Work with a partner. Discuss how the answers to Exercise 7 help
you to form a picture of the situation in the Belgian Congo at this
time.

9 Put the following in the order of Marlow's travels from the time he
is back in London after six years on the Indian Ocean, the Pacific
and the China Seas. Then choose three and talk about what
happens to Marlow there.

a his aunt's house ......

b Brussels ......

c the mouth of the River Congo ......

d London ......

e a 300-kilometre journey on foot ......

f the coast of West Africa ......

g the Central Station ......

10 At the beginning of his story, Marlow says, 'We are saved by our
commitment to efficiency.' Discuss how the following are good or
bad examples of European efficiency.

a the crew of the French battleship

b the conditions at the Outer Station and at the Central Station

c the Company's chief accountant

d the success of the manager at the Central Station

e the brickmaker

11 How are these pairs of things connected?
   a the Captain of the *Nellie* and the four other men on the ship
   b rivets and bricks
   c hippos and the Company's agents
   d the leader of the Eldorado Exploring Company and the manager of the Central Station
   e the River Thames and the River Congo
12 What do we know about Kurtz by the end of Chapter 1? What is he like? What do others think of him? What does he do?

Chapter 2

Before you read
13 What people and scenes surprise Marlow in Chapter 1? What kind of surprises do you expect him to face in this chapter?
14 In Chapter 1, Marlow meets a number of people in the Congo: the Swedish steamboat captain, the Company's chief accountant, the manager of the Central Station, a group of ambitious agents, the brick-maker, the mechanic, the manager's uncle. Who do you think will be important to the story in Chapter 2? Who will cause problems for Marlow?

While you read
15 What dangers do they face? Draw lines to the dangers on the right.
   a the manager   a spear
   b Kurtz   a screech from the steamboat's whistle
   c the agents   hunger
   d the steamboat   the climate
   e the cannibals   illness
   f the pilot   objects under the surface
   g the natives   Kurtz's power
16 Circle the correct endings.
   a Kurtz is
      – English.
      – French.
      – from all over Europe.

b Kurtz wrote an important
  – book.
  – report.
  – letter.
c Marlow
  – buries the pilot.
  – kills the pilot.
  – pushes the pilot's body into the river.
d The man who greets the steamer on its arrival at Kurtz's station is dressed
  – untidily.
  – in black.
  – in colourful clothes.
e The young man is
  – Dutch.
  – English.
  – Russian.
f The natives want
  – Kurtz to stay.
  – to kill Kurtz.
  – Kurtz to leave.

After you read

17 Marlow travels from the Central Station to the Inner Station. What happens in each of these places?

a at the Central Station
b on the steamboat at the beginning of the journey to the Inner Station
c 80 kilometres below the Inner Station and Kurtz
d 12 kilometres from the Inner Station
e 3 kilometres from the Inner Station
f at the Inner Station

18 Who is speaking? Who are they talking to, and what are they talking about?
   a 'The climate might solve the problem for you.'
   b 'Good God! What is the meaning of this?'
   c 'Catch them! Give them to us.'
   d 'Turn the wheel! Get her going straight again.'

19 After the pilot dies, Marlow thinks that Kurtz is probably dead, too. He talks about what he learned, much later, about Kurtz's actions and character. According to Marlow, are these statements true (T) or false (F)?
   a Kurtz's voice made people think he was a genius. .....
   b There were no women involved in Kurtz's life. .....
   c The Congo had greatly affected Kurtz and changed his way of thinking. .....
   d Kurtz was not interested in possessions. .....
   e Kurtz was a typical, common Englishman. .....
   f Kurtz joined in native customs and ceremonies. .....
   g Marlow admired most of Kurtz's report for the International Society for the Control of Savage Customs. .....
   h Kurtz always loved and respected the natives in the Congo. .....

Chapter 3

Before you read

20 If the young Russian is a typical, loyal admirer of Kurtz, how do you think the natives, who 'don't want Kurtz to go', will welcome Marlow and the other white men?

21 Think of two or three possible questions for Marlow to ask Kurtz when he finally has the opportunity to talk to him.

While you read

22 Who holds this opinion of Kurtz? Mark each statement **M** for Marlow or **R** for the young Russian. How are their opinions different?
   a Kurtz explains important topics very clearly. .....
   b Contact with Kurtz is something to be proud of. .....

c Kurtz is a thief. .....

d The natives love and respect Kurtz. .....

e Kurtz can commit murder without fear of punishment. .....

f Kurtz is mad and greedy. .....

g Kurtz is empty inside. .....

h The fact that Kurtz expects to be treated as a god
is horrifying. .....

i The heads outside Kurtz's house belong to rebels. .....

j Kurtz gives the observer the impression of death. .....

k Kurtz is truly a god. .....

23 Complete the sentences with the right people.

a .... orders the attack on the steamer.

b .... looks wild and wonderful.

c Mr Kurtz's good name is important to ....

d .... gives the young man some bullets.

e .... does not accept the rules of God or Man.

f As the boat, with Kurtz on board, moves downstream,
.... are ready to shoot the natives.

g Marlow gives .... some of Kurtz's private letters.

h .... believes that Kurtz spoke her name before he
died.

i .... lies to the young woman because he wants to
be kind to her.

After you read

24 In each pair, circle the word or words that give a more accurate
description.

a Kurtz:

(1) physically sick / physically well

(2) mentally ill / mentally healthy

(3) weak-minded / purposeful

(4) remarkable / dull

(5) a fool / a genius

(6) satisfied / ambitious

(7) confident / uncertain

(8) stupid / intelligent

    (9) a rebel / a Company man

    (10) generous / greedy

b the native woman:

    (1) ugly / beautiful

    (2) uneducated / educated

    (3) obedient / wild

    (4) proud / shy

    (5) queenly / common

    (6) plain / decorated

    (7) strong / weak

c the Intended:

    (1) truthful / dishonest

    (2) selfish / generous

    (3) loyal / false

    (4) dark / pale

    (5) deserving / uncaring

    (6) hopeful / tragic

    (7) cruel / kind

25 How does Conrad give the reader the impression that Marlow
has entered a nightmare on the night he follows Kurtz into the
jungle and returns to the steamboat with him? Consider lighting,
sounds, danger, ghosts, feelings – both physical and psychological
– Kurtz's voice, his words, his appearance.

26 During the journey down the river, back to the Central Station,
Marlow says, 'the ghost of the original Kurtz visited the bedside of
this false Kurtz'. Discuss the characters of these 'two Kurtzes' with
a partner. Can you connect his last words, 'The horror! The horror!'
to the two sides of Kurtz?

27 Marlow is uncomfortable with life in Brussels. Imagine an annoying
conversation that he hears in a coffee shop and act it out with a
partner. What would Marlow think if he heard your conversation?

28 Back in Brussels, Marlow has three visitors before he sees the
Intended. Which visitor (the first, second or third):

  a believes Kurtz was talented in several ways and has good
    memories of his cousin?

b believes Kurtz could persuade people and admires the political
   ideas Kurtz had?

   c believes the Company has a right to Mr Kurtz's papers and
   discoveries, and has a threatening attitude?

Writing

29 You are looking for actors to play the roles of Charlie Marlow and
   Kurtz in a new film of *Heart of Darkness*. Write descriptions of the
   two men you want for the roles.

30 You are the Manager of the Central Station. Write two pages from
   your diary for the trip by steamboat from your station to the Inner
   Station. Write about one event and about your opinion of the
   people around you.

31 Kurtz's family plan a service to honour him after his death. Write
   a speech for the service by the Intended, Charlie Marlow or an
   official from the Company.

32 Write a letter from Marlow to the Company doctor in Brussels. Tell
   him what you have seen that proves or disproves his scientific
   theory.

33 The Intended travels to Africa to see where Kurtz died, and she
   meets the beautiful native woman who Kurtz left behind. Imagine
   both women speak English and write a conversation between
   them.

34 The Company needs more agents in the Belgian Congo, but they
   do not want men like Kurtz who cause problems. What experience
   and qualities is the Company looking for? Write an advertisement
   for this job, to be placed in a British newspaper.

35 You are a magazine writer and have interviewed Marlow after he
   returns to Europe. Compare and contrast his opinion on the topic
   'Europe's role in Africa' with the opinion of Marlow's aunt and
   many Europeans.

36 You are a student taking a class in English literature. Make notes
   on Conrad's use of light and dark as you remember it from the
   story. Decide on a title for your paper.

37 Imagine that Kurtz returns to the Central Station on the steamboat and recovers his health. What will he do next? Write a different ending to the story.

38 You are reporting on *Heart of Darkness* for your book club. Decide how many stars to give it (out of five) and tell the members of your group why you recommend it or not.

WORD LIST

accounts (n) financial records; an accountant has the job of keeping or checking these

agent (n) a person who deals with someone else's business for them

anchor (n) a heavy metal object that is dropped into the water to prevent a ship or boat from moving

arrow (n) a thin, straight weapon with a point at one end

blindfold (n/v) a piece of cloth that covers someone's eyes so that they cannot see

candle (n) a stick of wax that you burn to produce light

cannibal (n) someone who eats human flesh

clown (n) someone who entertains people by dressing in unusual clothes, painting their face and doing funny things

colony (n) a country or area that is controlled by a more powerful country

conquer (v) to get control over a country, an enemy or your feelings by force; successful control is a **conquest**

crawl (v) to move on your hands and knees

deck (n) the flat top part of a ship or boat, which you can walk on

despair (n/v) a feeling of being very unhappy and without hope

exterminate (v) to kill all of a particular group of people

genius (n) someone who has an extremely high level of intelligence, artistic ability or skill at a particular activity

hippopotamus, hippo (n) a large African animal with a big head, fat body and thick grey skin that lives in or near water

horrify (v) to shock someone very much; something very shocking is **horrific**

intended (n) the person you plan to marry

ivory (n) the hard, smooth, yellow-white substance from the long outer tooth of an elephant

jungle (n) a large tropical forest with trees and large plants growing very close together

knit (v) to make clothes out of wool, using long thick needles to tie the wool together

monster (n) a large, ugly, frightening creature in stories; someone who is very cruel and evil

mourn (v) to feel very sad because someone has died

nightmare (n) a very frightening dream

rivet (n) a metal pin for connecting flat pieces of metal together

sacrifice (n/v) the act of giving up something important or valuable in order to get something

savage (n/adj) someone from a country where the way of living is simple and undeveloped (a word which is now offensive)

screech (n) a very high, loud, unpleasant noise

telescope (n) a tube-shaped piece of equipment that makes things that are far away seem closer and larger

trade (n/v) the activity of buying or selling large quantities of goods, especially between one country and another